The Art of Sandcastling

ROMAR BOOKS

The Art of
SANDCASTLING

TED SIEBERT

ROMAR BOOKS LTD.
Seattle, Washington

The Art of Sandcastling

Copyright © 1990 by Romar Books Ltd.

Published by Romar Books Ltd.
18002 15th Ave. NE, Suite B
Seattle, Washington 98155

First Edition

Printed and bound in Hong Kong

ISBN 0-945265-27-1

Front Cover: Sand sculpture and photo by David Henderson
1990 U.S. Navy Worldwide Conference,
San Diego, California

Back Cover: "Sunglasses and Visor" by the Sandyhands
Photograph by Warren Blakely
"Tower of the Branches" by Lars Van Nigtevegt
Photograph by Lars Van Nigtevegt
"Warrior" by Team Hardcore
Photograph by David Henderson
Ted Siebert, practicing for another contest
Photograph by Karen Duncan

Background Photograph by Barry Gregg, Seattle, Washington

Dedicated to the memory of my father,
Harlan A. Siebert

Contents

Walter McDonald

Acknowledgments

Much of the enjoyment in putting this book together came from meeting and speaking with sandcastling folks, the organizers of events as well as the builders themselves. They are too numerous for us to mention all who have contributed, but I am very grateful to everyone who donated time and entrusted me with photographs.

I would like to single out a few key individuals. To the north, in the greater Vancouver, British Columbia, area I would like to thank the members of three sandcastling teams: the Artisands des Dreams, Grain Assault, and Freddie and the Sandblasters. We've turned into a sort of big sandcastling family because of our mutual respect and admiration.

A number of Californians proved very helpful. Special thanks go to Skip Carlstrom, Gary Kinsella, Gerry Kirk, Mary Nichols, Jeff Smith, Mike Stewart, Kent Trollen, and Todd Vander Pluym.

In South Padre Island, Texas, those Sons of the Beach, "Amazing Walter" McDonald and "Sandy Feet" Wierenga, were a big help. The Sons of the Beach are also working on a book, and I wish them the best of luck. I also wanted to pass along the Sons of the Beach sandcastling pledge. Raise your right hand: "I promise to have fun, help others have fun, and unlitter."

In Florida, Marc and Susan Altamar of Daytona Beach provided a wealth of information.

In Atlantic City, Louis Levine and Bill McMahon furnished me with the historical information about the turn-of-the-century sandsculpting that took place off the boardwalk. Bill is currently writing a weekly column for the *Atlantic City Press* entitled "Historical Walks," essays on the history of south Jersey. He is also the author of *Atlantic City—So Young, So Gay*. Louis Levine, an accomplished artist, shared with me his experiences with the sand artists.

I even acquired a friend in Europe, Lars Van Nigtevegt of Holland. Although most of our communication has been by letter, I am grateful to be able to include his work. I was unable to include the work of his mentor, Pieter Wiersma, due to litigation stemming from his recent death, but I do agree with Lars: Pieter's work may be the best the world has ever seen.

At home in Seattle, I would like to thank the team Totally In Sand and the many people who have castled with us. There would not be a book without the efforts of Charlie Beaulieu, Russ Leno, and Noel West.

A very special thank you to Dave Henderson of Sand Sculptors International for the great photos and the phone calls. Dave has produced a video on sand sculpting; information about it appears in the appendix.

—— Introduction ——

When I was a boy growing up in Coeur d'Alene, Idaho, our family had the opportunity to do a lot of traveling. One of our favorite places to visit was the Oregon coast, and so I became aware of the Cannon Beach sandcastling contest at an early age. I remember seeing postcards and brochures of the winning entries. I particularly remember a replica of a Volkswagen bug that left me completely dumbfounded. My father was a sculptor, working mainly in cast iron, but these pieces were far different—imposing in their fragile nature, made entirely of sand and water. Although my hope that our family would someday stumble onto the contest was never fulfilled, as an adult I would have the opportunity to compete at Cannon Beach—and I jumped at the chance.

The five of us drove down from Seattle late one night. Our artistic talent consisted of my neighbor Russ Leno, a design engineer and an excellent wood carver, and my own experience. Our tools were archaic and our forms were even worse—some old fence boards that I had put together two days earlier. But our enthusiasm was never in doubt. We ventured onto the beach at seven the next morning.

Cannon Beach, with Haystack Rock anchored out in the Pacific Ocean, is a beautiful place; but on Sandcastle Day the beach takes

---

(Right) A sandcastle built at the contest in White Rock, British Columbia, by the Artisands des Dreams shortly after they organized as a team. *(Opposite)* A beautiful lion built for the Harrison Hot Springs contest by the Chisholm Town Cutters.

Artisands Des Dreams

on a new look. The National Guard was there, setting up registration tents and staking out plots, while wind socks the size of automobiles spun over our heads. There was even a tower lift for the television cameras. Some forty thousand people were expected to be on hand. "Forty *thousand*," we murmured. Russ and I looked at each other in amazement, calculating how many rows of Husky Stadium that number of people would fill.

The competition started at 8:00. We had four hours to work on our masterpiece—a Banff-Springs-type hotel. "It's this fabulous place in Alberta. Trust me, it'll look great," I kept saying. Unfortunately, I had forgotten to bring photographs, no one else on the team had seen the hotel, and it had been some time since I had been there.

However, we had gone down to have fun, and that we did. Within an hour, our plot was surrounded by spectators. By the second hour, they were standing ten deep. Some people had actually brought blankets and picnic lunches. They were not going to relinquish front row seats, even if it meant watching a novice group from Seattle. They had come for a show, and they got one. Next to us an Egyptian pyramid began to take shape, complete with costumes and that Steve Martin song "King Tut" playing over and over and over. On our other side, the *Titanic* was slowly resurfacing for yet another mishap. This structure would collapse, ironically, in the same spot in which the original had struck the iceberg.

Although we were disappointed with our results, when the contest ended we were besieged with questions. As much as they enjoyed watching us build, people were just as curious about our personal lives. "What do you do for a living?" "How long has your

Members of the team Totally in Sand practicing at Rockaway Beach, Oregon, at the end of the summer season.

group been castling?" That sort of thing. It was quite an experience to meet so many people who were actually interested in us. We enjoyed the attention so much that our group was one of the last to leave the beach.

Later that night we conducted a ceremonial burning of my forms. Russ and I vowed never again to do so poorly. Several months later, at a shopping mall parking lot on a very cold February day, we competed against two other men who also suffered from sandcastling fever—Charlie Beaulieu and Noel West. Eventually we formed a team called "Totally In Sand."

As much fun as it is to participate in, sandcastling is very much a spectator sport. Sandcastles demand to be seen. The four members of our team have sandboxes at home for practicing, and not a week goes by without one of us calling the others to race over and see a piece before it collapses.

Photographs won't do justice. Even when we practice at the beach, our work rarely lacks an audience. We hear the same two questions over and over again. "How do you get the sand to stay up?" and "Doesn't it make you sick to see all your hard work wash away?" But it's that last question that provides the real enigma: "Why do it?"

From an artistic point of view, working with such a delicate medium is pure joy. There are no toxic fumes to deal with, no real messes to clean up. Results are obtained quickly, yet there is the danger of partial or total collapse at any moment. There are no second chances; you must become completely absorbed in your work. The waves crashing on the beach and the sun warming your back provide a very creative atmosphere. At the risk of using a term as misunderstood as *abstract* is, sandcastling is probably the least abstract art form. The basic premise behind

The Orbital Sanders

(Above and following two pages) "Sandcastle Day" at Oregon's Cannon Beach, one of the most beautiful beaches in North America.

sandcastling is to make something easily recognizable from virtually nothing. Castling prompts people to ask questions about my fine arts background, which I like much better than discussing how my dog's wagging tail was used as a paint brush for a certain piece. As Walter McDonald, a professional sandcastler from South Padre Island, Texas, put it: "Building a sandcastle is like buying a rose. You do it for the beauty of the moment."

Sandcastling, besides being a lot of fun, is a thinking person's sport. Twenty percent of the contests listed in this book are sponsored by local chapters of the American Institute of Architects. I asked Skip Carlstrom, an architect from Fresno who heads the contest in that area, why so many architects are intrigued by sandcastling. He replied that sandcastling represents exactly what architectural planning is all about: working within the limitations of a singular building material. "Once you've graduated from the bucket-and-shovel type of sandcastling, it represents all sorts of engineering and design problems. How much mass can that structure safely hold? What percentage of water is actually used? How sheer can you go? And sight restrictions and weather conditions become a planning factor."

Jeff Smith, an architect who heads the A.I.A. contest at Corona Del Mar, adds that castling is also great publicity for architectural firms. "It shows the public that architects are alive and well—that we have personalities, and don't just sit around behind closed doors planning on ripping up the planet any further." I might add that an anonymous architect mentioned how nice it is to build something on the brink of disaster and not have to worry about a lawsuit on Monday.

But sandcastling is more than just showing off artistic and engineering talents; it also promotes camaraderie and helps develop the

The delight of children sandcastling at the annual Beach Festival at Hampton Beach, New Hampshire.

ability to work as a team. It is a rare sandcastling team that has a "star," one member who stands out in the public attention. Sandcastling is truly a team effort in both planning and building stages. Everyone understands the time factor and works closely together, and this spirit of working together can carry over into one's job or home.

It is a sport rich in tradition, history, and folklore. Once the sandcastling muse kicks in, people who would not normally crack open a book for enjoyment find themselves poring over volumes on architecture and art history.

Someday the public will grow tired of tractor-pulling and wrestling extravaganzas, steroid scandals and overpaid professional athletes. Sandcastling is becoming increasingly popular. And fortunately it has been around for a long time, long enough not to be considered a mere fad. Sandcastling does not require great athleticism, is relatively inexpensive, and appeals to all ages. It does not pollute the environment, provides great exercise for the body and mind, and is a virtual fountain of youth. It brings out the kid in everyone.

Sure, it hurts to see your piece wash away, but there's always another beach, another day. In fact, if it weren't for the high tide, we'd be bringing tiki torches and lanterns to the beach so we could castle all night. Someday a beach will sponsor a "castle 'til you drop contest." And I know of fifty people, offhand, who will be there. To borrow a line from the French artist Georges Rouault, "Art is never finished, only abandoned."

The intensity of adults giving shape to a sphinx in progress at the LEAP Sandcastle Contest held at San Francisco's Aquatic Park.

—History of Sandcastling—

Historians cannot tell exactly when a person—possibly a child—first sat on a beach and created a sand sculpture. We do know that the ancient Egyptians built sand replicas of their pyramids and monuments more than four thousand years ago, using their "sandcastles" the same way that architects now use cardboard models for their projects.

Building in sand became popular in the United States in the late 1800s. Sculptors known as "sand artists" worked along the famed boardwalk in Atlantic City, New Jersey, from 1897 to 1944. James Taylor was among the first to set up one of these open-air studios. Taylor was no ordinary sand artist in terms of technique and talent. He incorporated popular themes into his sculptures, executing caricatures of current presidents and other newsworthy figures;

The Sand Modeler   One of the Beach Innovations of Recent Years
Atlantic City, N. J.

(Above) A postcard (circa 1897) of James Taylor, who is considered to be America's first serious sand sculptor, working on a very relaxed figure in Atlantic City, New Jersey. *(Opposite)* The first sandcastle that master builder Gary Kinsella participated in building (1976).

on slow news days, he recreated famous art works and religious scenes. Attired in his dark suit and top hat, he was sure to remind passersby that donations were gladly accepted. He often inscribed "Don't forget the worker" and other sayings in the sand. Taylor has now become a cult figure for many serious builders.

Other artists followed Taylor's lead, and sand sculpturing became a lucrative business for a handful of these sand artists. There were generally no more than half a dozen of these artists working, building in pits to protect their sculptures from the wind and rain. A sand artist would be tossed nickels and dimes here and there, and by the 1930s could earn up to fifty dollars a week for his services.

The wind and rain have always been a sandcastler's worst enemies. This was especially true for the Atlantic City artists. They discovered that if they mixed one part cement with three parts sand, their sculptures would survive weather conditions better, and they could spend less time sculpting. The real money to be made was in sketching, particularly quick portraits for people on the boardwalk.

By the late 1930s, the original sand artists had retired to other projects and endeavors. The sand artists had been replaced by con artists. They used the sand sculptures in the pits to lure people off the boardwalk. Once he had them in his "studio," the artist could persuade people to have their portraits done. This sales pitch

A postcard (circa 1920) of a sand sculpture in Atlantic City. By this time the sand artists had begun adding cement to the sand as well as incorporating actual props into their sculptures.

became a scam when the portraits *never* looked like the subjects. Some of the artists would simply fill in a few details on printed silhouettes, much like those in a child's coloring book.

Back then the businesses adjacent to the boardwalk owned the property rights down to the sea, but were not allowed to build anything permanent on the beach side. The sand artists could get away with their racket because their sculptures were not considered permanent. The sand artists even enticed art students to do their sketches for them in exchange for twenty to thirty percent of the take.

This practice continued until 1944, when a hurricane hit the beach and leveled the pits. After that a city ordinance banned the artists from the beach.

The sport of sandcastling dates back to 1952, when the first contest was held in Fort Lauderdale, Florida. Like many contests, the Fort Lauderdale competition began as a family event for the Fourth of July festivities. The contest has since grown to include one hundred entries annually.

But it was on the west coast that sandcastling as a sport was first taken seriously. Several contests were born in the early sixties: Newport Beach, 1962; Alameda, Cannon Beach, and Carmel, 1964. Now considered the "granddaddies" of today's events, these contests are still going strong in the nineties.

The Cannon Beach contest was started after a tidal wave from the 1964 Alaska earthquake washed up Ecola Creek and took out the north bridge. Cannon Beach became

Newport Beach Chamber of Commerce

The Newport Beach Contest, sponsored by the Commodores Club and the Newport Beach Chamber of Commerce, was established in 1962, making it one of the oldest contests in North America.

11

a dead-end town. When the bridge was rebuilt in a new location, local merchants found that their business fell off, since the community was no longer easily accessible from Highway 101. They began the contest as a family event to draw people back to the beach. Sandcastle Day at Cannon Beach is now the community's largest tourist attraction, attended by over 1,000 contestants and tens of thousands of onlookers every year.

Other popular contests have come and gone. The most famous of these was the Canadian Open, held at White Rock, British Columbia. At a gathering one evening in the late 1970s, a handful of local people toyed with the idea of a sandcastling contest to increase local business and promote goodwill. They soon raised $5,000 in prize money, and five weeks later the first contest

was held. The Canadian Open came to be regarded as the world championship by many professional sandcastlers. In fact, the very popularity of the contest forced the community to call it off after 1987. That year the community of White Rock hosted 135 teams and more than 250,000 visitors. It proved too much for this small town in southwest British Columbia.

Sandcastling contests have become an important economic force for beach communities that rely heavily on summer tourism. Sandcastling appeals to all ages, and although the ideal weather for sandcastling would be a clear, sunny day, sandcastling contests will still draw crowds when the skies are overcast and grey.

The sport owes a large part of its success to the efforts of some key individuals

Like Hollywood's era of epics, sandcastling also had its period of epic-size sculptures. The Acropolis *(above)* was built in 1981, and Carracason *(preceding two pages)* was built in 1976 at Cardiff by the Sea, California. (Photos by Gerry Kirk)

from southern California. These people have helped raise the art of sandcastling to new levels of scale and sophistication. They include Gary Kinsella, Gerry Kirk, Norman Kraus, and Todd Vander Pluym, who built in the 1970s what came to be called "Labor Day Weekend Masterpieces." Works like the Heidelberg Castle, Mont-Saint-Michel, Bluebeard's Castle, and the Lost City of Atlantis were enormous projects that required dozens of sand artists and tons of sand and water.

These pieces were not only gigantic, but they were carved with such detail and accuracy that they have set the standards other groups still follow. Many of the techniques and tools used today were first conceived of and used by these artists, particularly Todd Vander Pluym. These folks have also inspired and helped others start their own sandcastling contests. Sandcastlers in the future will regard these people as pioneers in much the same way that we think of James Taylor today.

Gerry Kirk

Another sandcastle built in the epic period of sandcastles, "The Lost City of Atlantis" at one time held a world record for height. This fifty-two-foot-tall castle, complete with laser light show, was built by Sand Sculptors International at Treasure Island, Florida.

—— *Beginning Sandcastling* ——

Castling and sculpting on the beach begins with sand. Its grain size, silt content, and how many pebbles, shell fragments, and pieces of seaweed it contains will dictate what you can do with it. When mixed with water, clean sand becomes quite a cohesive material. A drop or two of moisture in an hourglass will ruin the timepiece forever. Part of what holds sand sculptures together is the surface tension created by mixing sand and water. The best way to explain this tension is to imagine two panes of glass stacked one on top of the other. Place a few drops of water between the two panes and they will become extremely difficult to separate; they will hold together as long as the panes remain moist.

Most sand consists largely of silica, a nonmetallic element that behaves in the same way as the two panes of glass. The shape of the sand grain and the silt contained in the sand cause it to act like a sponge, absorbing and holding water. In fact, a very high silt content will cause the sand to retain too much water, and it will not be able to support as much weight.

Sandcastles and sculptures require a lot of water to keep the sand, and therefore the structure, "sticking together." Sea water is the ideal bonding agent for a sandcastle. As

(Right) A sandcastle, built in competition, that towers over fifteen feet in height. *(Opposite)* A young boy works on his masterpiece.

sea water in a sculpture evaporates, salt crystals remain, forming a thin crust over the entire surface. If the sculpture is sprayed from time to time, an additional buildup of salt crystals will help preserve the piece.

Besides creating surface tension, adding water to sand causes a chemical reaction. Seawater or fresh water, when mixed with sand, creates an ionic bond. Ionic bonding is the attraction of positively and negatively charged particles, as opposed to covalent bonding, which is the sharing of electrons. Ionic bonding is a weak electrical force, except directly at the surface, but it is strong enough to help hold together packed and sculptured sand. A more detailed description of this bonding process appears in the appendix.

There are always concessions to make when selecting a plot to sandcastle on. Building above the high-tide line will require more time and energy in carrying water. Building below the tide line will shorten the life of the piece considerably.

The ideal location is just above the high-tide line. Deciding exactly where the high tide will peak is not always that easy. Normally, the previous high tide will leave a line of debris and foam stain. However, there is no guarantee that the tide will not roll in higher on the next cycle, or throw a freak wave at you, flooding your sculpture and sending your tools and forms surfing down the beach.

Santa Barbara Chamber of Commerce

(Above) The Volkswagen Bug is often the subject for the sand sculptor, along with dragons and castles. *(Following page)* A sandcastle competition sponsored by the School of Architecture at the University of Hawaii. Digging the hole for the inverted pyramid required more care than carving the above-ground pyramid because the weight of the sculptor could easily cause the sides to cave in.

When the site is selected, mark off boundaries. This precaution will not register with even the most intelligent unleashed dog, but it might cause a few kids to walk around. As fascinated as children generally are with sandcastling, some of them seem strangely compelled to pummel the sand sculpture or castle as soon as they can reach it.

Consider the position of the sun before you begin to build. Sculptures that face away from a setting sun will cast shadows that make photographing them difficult. If, however, the sun shines directly on your work, no shadow is cast and the effect of carved details can be lost.

In practicing for a competition, measure the plot according to the rules. Think of the plot as a canvas that must be filled with the image. Envision all four sides of the sculpture, as well as the center. Judges have a tendency to shave off points if the finished sculpture does not fit its plot size.

If you or your group are new to sandcastling, don't assume that you need a truckload of equipment to get started. You will need shovels and buckets, a few carving tools, and an idea. Keep a close watch on the smaller tools, though; they can become buried in no time.

Begin by mounding up sand to form a volcano shape, adding water at the top so it will drain into the center. The water will spread through the structure as it percolates down to the water table. Water should be added regularly as the mound grows. This

Sandcastling requires a lot of shoveling. In a four-hour contest, it is not unusual for a person to shovel over a ton of sand.

saturation helps to compact the sand. And, of course, jumping up and down on the mound will certainly help compact it.

Shovelling sand is strenuous work, especially wet sand on the tide flats. The average sandcastler shovels more sand in one day of competition than a full-time gardener moves in a month. The amount of shovelling required depends on the size of the piece. However, the energy used by the novice sandcastler is often more than double that of more experienced competitors. There is a correct way to shovel.

The first secret is to avoid using small shovels. Reaching far down with a small shovel will ruin the lower back in no time. Another pitfall to avoid is digging a large hole. The deeper the hole, the shorter your shovel becomes. And later on, the hole will probably have to be filled in. If it's too close to the sculpture, it can undermine the piece as the hole spreads from erosion.

Keep the actual motion of the shovelling fluid, much the way a baseball is thrown. Simply sticking the spade straight down and throwing the load with the strength in your arms creates a lot of work. For dry sand, the shoveling motion should be an even effort from scooping to throwing. On tide flats, it's better to break off chunks of sand, working in a circular pattern, moving away from your sculpture. By outlining your composition beforehand, you can identify places where the sand should remain intact. Then you won't have to fill those places in later.

After the sand has been mounded and it feels solid, the next step is to carve. In

Ann Chamberlain

Carving as a team requires good organization, as in the case of this group in San Francisco.

Noel West

attempting a sand sculpture, you must think of the design as being hidden, as if it had a blanket thrown over it, waiting to come out.

Sandcastling is a process of whittling away, and it must begin at the top, proceeding down. Time and energy spent on work below an unfinished top is futile. The sand from the top will fill in the lower detail as it falls away from the structure.

Start with the big tools and progress to the smaller detailing tools. The goal is to reduce the weight of the structure while keeping a pyramidal shape for support. Although castling begins from the top down, the actual motion of carving is not always from top to bottom. Carving from the bottom up reduces fractures and offers more control over the work. Working in a downward motion can sometimes lead to reckless mistakes, as gravity tends to pull down on the carving hand.

Unless you are battling a gale-force wind, it is very important to keep the structure as balanced as possible. If you carve away from one side, do the same to the other side, working down to a rough shape. Often a soon-to-be-frustrated carver will whittle a spire down to nothing, or undercut one side, ensuring an eventual collapse.

Knowing where and when to undercut requires practice. For example, a dragon's tail is cylindrical. If it is lying on the ground, it touches on a smaller surface plane than if it were flat on the bottom. Building the tail of a dragon with this in mind, you have to round the bottom as well as the top. It does not have to be undercut greatly, but the more correctly it is carved, the more realistic it

Wet sand shovels in clumps and needs to be broken up in the same way grapes used to be crushed in wineries.

will look when light and shadow fall on it. To undercut the tail, sink a flat tool an inch or so into the bottom of the mounded tail at ground level. As you move the tool upward, decrease pressure and follow the tail's shape to the top. By moving your tool upward, you will be keeping the sand packed, reducing the possibility of collapse.

In carving straight walls, it is important to keep your tools at a consistent angle. Hold your tool steady and keep the motion fluid. Carve to a rough outline where details protrude, and take the sand away from the outside of your marks.

Adventuresome carvers love to carve things to the verge of collapse. If you don't care for that risk, you can cut your piece only deep enough so that the shadows will fill in the depressions, creating the same effect as deep carving.

Hollowing out tunnels and building sheer walls will always impress the judges, and they are just plain fun to do. The trick is to avoid collapse. Begin with simple, safe shapes. As your experience grows, your technique will improve. A bullet-shaped arch is the safest arch to begin with. Reducing the weight of your arch by tapering on certain planes will greatly reduce the load your supports must bear.

Mounding sand in a volcano-like form is the most common method of building the basic structure. Working with forms is another, and will be discussed in detail in the following chapter. The third method is drip castling.

David Henderson

Carving sandcastles normally requires that the work start from the top to bottom. However, there are times when carved pieces can be added after the basic sculpture has been carved. The steeples in the above photograph were placed on the castle after the rest of the carving had been completed.

23

Drip castling uses supersaturated sand, the consistency of pancake batter, that can be run through your fist. Drip sandcastles are interesting compositions, although castlers usually tend to use the technique to build decorations on a larger work. Trees, for example, can be dripped very effectively. To drip a structure, take some wet sand in your fist, open your little finger, and let the wet sand run through, forming a stalagmite. On beaches with a high silt content, one can actually build tall spires and structures using this method. A related technique is similar to the way a child makes mud pies: the wet sand is jostled together in your hands and stacked. Build slowly and allow time for the water to drain before adding more sand pies.

For a complicated drip arch, the two spires are joined in the center with the back of one hand bridging the arch, while the other drips the sand to form the keystone. Once in position, the hand can be removed. This takes practice.

If a carved figure can stand on its own for a few minutes, it will probably last the

David Watersun

Dragons are a popular sand sculpting theme. *(Above)* A detailed Hawaiian dragon compliments of master builder Billy Lee. *(Opposite, above)* A dragon from Oklahoma busies himself in front of a televsion. *(Opposite, below)* The head of a very long dragon in progress—1.5 miles at Long Beach, Washington.

duration of the sculpture. If a structure actually collapses, repairs can sometimes be made. Other times, the piece will have to be reconstructed. Vertical stress cracks can appear on a major structure after a partial collapse; these lines must be V-notched out to prevent their spreading. Horizontal cracks pose a more serious threat, since they represent an avalanche waiting to happen. Gravity is encouraging the entire structure to slide off. The crack must be notched at both ends and the weight on top greatly reduced.

Sandcastling as a team presents its own challenges. Contests are often several driving hours away. The team must practice for major competitions, so meetings must be called, tools organized, and team members made aware of their roles. A captain should be appointed. Ideally, a group should consist of a bunch of artistic types who can shovel three cubic yards of sand at a time, pack water like mules, and do it all with smiles on their faces. There are few breaks taken in a four-hour contest. The amount of energy expended in the last half hour of a competition is amazing!

Finally, whether you've built a sculpture for your own entertainment or for show, it's always fun to watch the tide come in and take it away. Get some photos of it now. It won't be there tomorrow!

Lars Van Nigtevegt

David Henderson

(Above) Double archway sculpted by Lars Van Nigtevegt of the Netherlands. *(Right)* A beautiful example of a hollow dome in which the sculptor, Dave Henderson, used inflatable toys to create the hollows. *(Opposite)* Coke bottle in the pop art tradition, carved in British Columbia.

— Sandcastling with Forms —

A sandcastling form can be a simple bucket turned upside down or a specially constructed wooden box. Forms are essential for building structures that are very sheer or very tall. They serve two purposes in sandcastling: they allow the sand to be packed in a confined space, and they allow water to supersaturate the sand. Whatever its size or shape, the form must be able to keep its shape when filled with sand, as well as be able to support the weight of the forms placed above it.

When using buckets as forms, there are a few rules that must be followed. Buckets you intend to stack should be a series of graduated sizes; their bottoms must be removed; and the base that they rest on must be level. For buckets larger than five gallons,

we recommend you keep a half-inch border of the original bottom intact to help them retain their shape under pressure. If you plan to use garbage cans, we recommend the higher-quality plastics such as Rubbermaid brand, since the material is very durable and smooth.

Some buckets are useless for sandcastling because their walls are too flexible; the sand will not set up properly in them. This type of bucket can be improved considerably by wrapping duct tape around the outside, or by reinforcing it with fiberglass. Buckets with ridges along the inside wall are not recommended. The ridges can make the bucket difficult to remove from the molded sand.

Pictured below is a series of buckets

(Above) Sandcastling with forms allows the sand to become supersaturated as well as tightly packed in a confined space. (Opposite) Using a cone to make teeth for a very large dragon.

29

as forms, beginning with a common five-gallon bucket. Sand and water are layered in each bucket in stages. We normally begin by filling the bottom bucket with water, and then add sand to that. Pay close attention to the edges. Run your hands along the edge to reduce the development of air pockets. Otherwise, your finished sand tower will have a marbled appearance. Continue this process until the bucket is filled.

The sand does not have to be as wet as you might think. If drainage is a problem on your plot, you might consider mixing the sand and water before filling the bucket, rather than adding sand and water in layers.

If the sand is cluttered with seaweed, rocks, or shells, it's a good idea to screen out the debris ahead of time.

Although using soaking-wet sand will not harm your bucket tower, the buckets should be allowed to stand a few minutes to allow the excess water to drain. This decrease in water weight greatly reduces the load the bottom form must support, and the drainage allows for some natural settling and packing. Sand that is too wet does not carve well, since its cohesive strength is reduced.

When your bucket tower is complete, carefully tap along the outside of the top bucket. This is to break the seal between the

(Above) Like mushrooms springing up overnight, these sandcastles (in progress) appeared after just five hours of competition at Harrison Hot Springs, British Columbia. The sand is so good there that these castles remained standing for several weeks after the weekend contest had ended. *(Opposite)* The final forms of the center piece of the 2.85 mile-long sandcastle at Myrtle Beach, South Carolina.

bucket and the wet sand, leaving the compacted sand undisturbed. Smaller buckets require little or no tapping, while larger ones require considerably more. (Use a shovel to pry at the base of large forms such as garbage cans.) Once the seal is broken, the form should come off with little resistance. Carefully remove the form, keeping it as straight as possible. Once the top form is removed, we recommend rough-carving some of the sand away before pulling off too many more buckets. A four-foot tower with a fifteen-inch base is often too sheer to stand unless some of the weight is removed right away.

Working with complicated molds and super-sheer cones requires a different technique; they are generally the last ones used and are filled from the bottom, then turned over and lifted into place. It is necessary to cut an opening in the top of a cone-shaped form so that the water will drain while the form is being filled. This opening comes in handy for removing a difficult form like a transmission fluid funnel, since air blown through the neck does a wonderful job of breaking the seal.

Having recently acquired a forty-two-inch cone with an eight-and-a-half-inch base, our gang of sand-addicts couldn't wait to try it out; it would add a good two feet to our castles without our having to construct any additional forms. But after several tries and as many collapses, it became apparent that the angle of the cone was too steep. The filled

Using forms in the construction of a sandcastle requires that carving proceed from the top to the bottom.

cone weighed approximately 130 pounds, and it took two of us to lift it carefully into place while a third person covered the bottom to keep the sand from falling out. We tried several types of sand and various packing techniques, but the result was collapse after collapse. Not willing to accept defeat graciously, we resorted to cutting the cone into thirds, and stacking the pieces. Also, we began searching for an identical cone to reinforce with fiberglass and experiment with further.

For both molds and cones, the sand has to be packed carefully. Sand that is too wet will stick to the molds; sand that is too dry will not hold up. If the consistency of the sand-water mixture is perfect, the sand will slip out of the mold with little or no tapping or blowing. The advantage of using these "finished" forms is the time saved in carving, since the shape is generally finished. However, the judges in some contests frown on their use, and it would be advisable to find this out ahead of time.

Wet, compacted sand weighs approximately 125 pounds per cubic foot. Sandstone weighs about 138 pounds per cubic foot. Finding ready-made forms larger than a garbage can that can withstand this kind of pressure can be difficult and expensive. You may have to construct the forms yourself.

The same rules that apply to using buckets apply to working with constructed forms. The forms must be placed on a level surface. They must retain their shape while being filled with compacted sand, and must be able to support the weight of the forms placed on top of them. Side boards called wailers (normally two-by-fours) should be used as reinforcement in the construction of any sand-

United Way's "History of Architecture" in sand required the use of many forms.

The sandcastling forms used by the Artisands Des Dreams from Vancouver, British Columbia. The team uses a combination of tapered and square forms. A four-sided shell tapers in, with side boards attached. This tapering means less sand will be used, which requires less shoveling. Once the form is filled, four shovels can pop the seal. The entire structure can be lifted off intact, reducing the time spent reconstructing it. This is something that can't be done with completely square boxes.

Totally In Sand

The team Orbital Sanders from Seattle, Washington, uses a more standard type of form. Eight-inch round eyebolts are placed in each corner. Both rectangles and squares can be built this way. Two-by-fours run along the top and bottom to prevent bowing. A banding strip holds the entire structure together. The bolts are pulled, the strip cut, and the form peeled off.

The Orbital Sanders

Marc Jacobson

Pictured here are forms used by the team Totally in Sand. Charlie Beaulieu, a general contractor, came up with a unique idea. Rather than build square boxes with ninety-degree angles, he chose to build his forms in the shape of a hexagon, reducing the corner angle to sixty degrees. He also reduced the vertical angle of inclination from ninety degrees to seventy-seven degrees. The six-sided shape allows the weight of the sand to be more evenly distributed. Three-quarter-inch concrete form boards, which are specially treated on one side, are used instead of plywood. The edges are dadoed, creating a water-tight seal. Concrete snap ties and two-by-fours ride along the midsection. To hold the form together, we start with screws an inch and a quarter long, four per side. To compensate for wear, longer screws (up to two and a half inches long) replace the smaller ones with each outing. Once a hole is exhausted, a new one is drilled. The original hole is then puttied over. Using a cordless screwdriver, we can pull the form off in two pieces. The pieces are interchangeable so that different shapes can be formed, and the forms can easily be broken down for traveling.

castling form. The corners may be secure, but if the sideboards bow, your sculpture will turn into a disaster. Although it may appear solidly packed, the sand will develop stress cracks or collapse immediately after the form is released. When not in use, forms should be stacked on a level base so they will not warp.

No matter which forms are used, it is important to be able to reuse them. All the previously-mentioned forms have been used in many contests and practices. Avoid using nails to hold corners together. Prying nails off can disturb the compacted sand, and rarely do sixteen-penny nails all go in straight and come out clean. Having someone step on a nail can ruin an outing. Also avoid using particleboard and lower-grade plywood, neither of which is structurally sound. To insure a water-tight seal, many teams staple a flap of plastic over the corners.

Collapse is the dirtiest word in sandcastling. The best forms in the world will not support the sand if it is not packed correctly. In sandcastling, many contests take place below the high-tide line, which may seem to the novice to be a source of instant packed sand. Simply shoveling wet sand does *not* pack it, even though it might appear solid.

Wet sand is shoveled in clumps, and needs to be broken up—usually by the same method people once used to crush grapes for wine. Unless the sand clumps are broken up, air pockets will develop, and the packed sand will resemble Swiss cheese. Lots of water will help resolve this problem, but if you're trying to attain extreme height or attempting

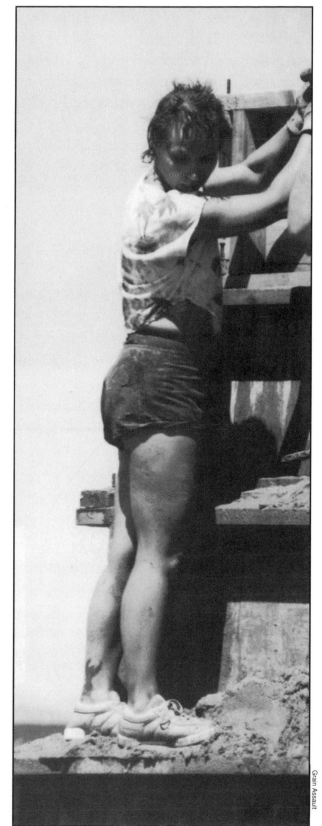

Grain Assault

Sandcastling forms, when graduated sufficiently, can serve as a ladder. The sand should be periodically brushed away from the ledges to allow for proper footing.

an engineering feat, a packing device is necessary.

A packing device is anything with enough thrust and weight to create sandstone if applied over a period of time. A well-packed form will sound solid when it is being compressed, and a packer can send tremors through the entire plot. Packing is also very strenuous work. It can exhaust the person driving the pile in a short amount of time. It's a good idea to take turns driving the pile, and to be extremely careful not to hit toes or the edges of the forms.

A good rule of thumb is to saturate your base by filling it with water six to eight inches deep. Add sand until the water is completely absorbed by the sand. As the sand-water mixture settles, it's time to pack. Water and sand are then added in six- to eight-inch increments, packed, and then the process is repeated until the desired height is achieved. As with the bucket tower, the base must be level. We usually take a level with us, since most ocean beaches are on a slant.

In constructing and filling a very large form, time can be saved by sinking the first form into the ground as if it were a cookie cutter. The dimensions of the bottom form are outlined in the sand and a trench is dug. Then the form is settled into the trench; it has been effectively "pre-filled." Digging the required two- to three-foot-deep trench will

(Below and opposite page) The pyramidal shape of the wizard reduces the weight that the base must support.

Fred Dobbs

require that some of the sand be tossed outside rather than inside your form outline. Otherwise, the team will fight a losing battle with the mountain of sand formed in the middle. We estimate half an hour of digging time can be saved this way, and nobody enjoys digging sand all day if they can help it.

Two problems can occur with your forms. Either the side boards will bow or a corner will give way (a blowout). Provided the corners can be secured, a blowout poses no real threat. Although it's not very pretty, a corner brace can stabilize the movement.

A bow in your forms, however, presents an entirely different problem. Even if the corners remain intact, a serious bow represents a form that is in a state of expansion, and no amount of packing can guarantee the solidity of the compacted sand. You are putting in more sand than the form is designed to hold. Side boards are critical in constructing forms holding more than a cubic yard of sand.

If you're planning to build a very tall structure, it's a good idea to step each form in a few inches or so as you work your way up. Then the forms can serve as a ladder as well. Working at fifteen feet or higher, one definitely needs a good foothold.

Some words about safety are in order here. A while back we were castling at Cannon Beach on an unusually hot day. Next to us was a group of women from the University of Oregon. About an hour into the contest, one of them collapsed. We assumed she was suffering from the heat, and since

there were several people tending to her, we went back to work. After the contest we discovered that one of her friends had shoveled her toenail off! Ouch!

Accidents can happen anywhere. Normally, they aren't any one person's fault, but usually they can be avoided. Stepping on a nail poking through an unused form or getting dinged in the head by an overzealous shoveler are injuries that need not happen. Safety is not just the responsibility of the captain, but of everyone on the team. If a tool is not being used and will not fit into your pouch, it has no place in the plot. Someone suffering from a back problem should not be doing any heavy lifting.

Our group has been fortunate in avoiding any serious injuries; but as our castles grow taller and taller, we have been concerned about someone falling off the top due to poor footing or heat exhaustion. This is a frequent topic of discussion at our meetings. People who do not take proper precautions are not invited back to sandcastling contests.

When you sandcastle, you should always have plenty of fluids to drink, have sun

Great care should be exercised when sandcastling, particularly on hot days when the sun can drain the energy and burn the skin. Heat stroke is not an uncommon problem at sandcastle contests.

screen available, and wear some type of foot protection. Sunglasses are a good idea, at least while the first forms are being filled, since so much sand and water sloshes around. The use of gloves is highly recommended to prevent blisters and to avoid slivers while packing the forms. Any sharp edges or metallic protrusions on the forms should be sanded down.

But the sun is the most frequent source of injuries. Serious sunburn and exhaustion are a real danger. Fair-skinned sandcastlers should bring clothing that covers their necks as well as their backs, and should bring along some sun block. Any medical conditions should be mentioned to the captain of the team in case of an emergency.

Carving into a mountain of sand, as fun as it is, can also be dangerous, and should never be attempted alone. There is no advance warning of a cave-in. It can happen so quickly and quietly that, unless you have friends working beside you, no one may know you're missing until it's too late.

Grain Assault

Carving into the side of a mountain or quarry of sand should never be done alone. Too much undercutting can trigger an avalanche of sand in a matter of seconds.

—— Sandcastling Tools ——

Sand is such a soft medium that almost anything will work as a tool for carving and shaping it. Of course, sandcastlers need shovels. The small ones with handles require too much effort for too little result. Use the long-handled, pointed ones. The flat shovels sometimes used in construction work are good for moving dry sand and are handy to have on hand for cutting walls.

Unless you're working on tide flats, your sandcastle will require that you carry a lot of water. Normally, you'll want to have five-gallon buckets for hauling water. Carrying anything larger requires a Herculean effort. Our team usually brings about eighty buckets to major competitions and fills them before the contest begins. Finding buckets is not difficult. Painting contractors go through many of the big, white plastic ones, and will gladly give you their empties. Be sure to clean them out before using them at the beach, since the paint flakes will pollute the beach. Stacked buckets can be a nightmare to pull apart, and we normally rub sand on the outside before we stack them.

Garden sprayers and misters are necessary as well. The canister-type sprayers are used to keep the sculptures moist, preserving the detail. (Please do not use a sprayer that has been used for pesticides.) Smaller misters like the ones used on house plants will also work, but you'll almost certainly get a cramp in your hand after using them for a short while. Misters are great for spraying color with water-based paint. Be sure to use only non-polluting paints.

Marc Jacobson

The Orbital Sanders

Simply shoveling sand into a form will not pack the sand. A packing device *(opposite and lower right)* is necessary to avoid the risk of collapse. Even a foot *(upper right)* will work.

To say the tips of sprayers have a tendency to clog on the beach is an understatement. And the clog always seems to happen when you most need the spray. The best way to prevent this is to keep your sprayer tip submerged in water when it's not in use. A clogged sprayer is not only a nuisance, but a large drop of water can ruin the most delicately carved piece.

If you're going to raid your kitchen utensil drawer, keep in mind that those famous words *stainless steel* lose their meaning when implements are exposed to sea water. If metal tools are not rinsed with fresh water after a day of sandcastling, they will begin rusting almost immediately. With the excep-

tion of a few dental tools and my Holbein palette knife, every tool we have has long since turned brown.

Tools rust quickly, but they can become buried even faster. Our team seems to lose something on every outing. Buried tools are a chore to find, and they can be dangerous. Step on a garden rake once with a bare foot and you'll agree. If a tool is not being used, or cannot fit into a pouch or box, it should be set outside the plot in a safe place.

What might be the most useful sandcastling tool manufactured is the palette knife. Originally intended as a tool to mix oil paint, the knife is a necessity for sandcastling. The steel is thin and flexible and can cut perfect

Carving columns with an "instant pillar." Specialized tools can greatly reduce the time it takes to create such a piece.

shapes without disturbing the sand you want to leave intact. They come in several shapes and sizes. Buy a cheap shovel, but buy a palette knife that is quality stainless steel. It will remain the shiniest tool in your collection.

There are probably a lot of tools lying around your house that would work as sandcastling tools, including trowels, spatulas, melon ballers, and so forth. You needn't invest a bundle of money. Amazingly useful tools are relatively easy to make.

Detailing a Greco-Roman structure, for instance, becomes a quick and easy task with an "instant pillar." (All our favorite tools have names.) It is nothing more than a piece of laminate that has been drilled with a straight, close row of large, uniform holes, and cut in half to form two scalloped tools. Pillars can be carved freehand, of course, but with this tool they can be etched in ten minutes.

Forming columns takes about three swipes of the instant pillar. The first swipe creates the general shape. The second and third swipes, which are shorter, create bulkheads and clear the sand in between. If you want clean or perfect columns, use the tool from the bottom to the top. If you desire a ruins-type appearance, run the tool from the top to the bottom.

Laminate, cut into various shapes, can

Pieces of banding material are duct-taped together to form "hoops" for carving uniform detail.

45

do amazing things. Our team has "instant shake roof," "instant belly," "instant scale," and "instant spire," for example. Pieces of laminate are also handy for making templates for outlining perfectly shaped doors and windows. Cut into simple rectangles and squares, the laminate can be used to cut clean edges. It also works well for cleaning out large amounts of sand, and its light weight gives good control over the work. Slightly thinner and more flexible pieces are great for cutting larger shapes or symmetrical edges.

Another tool that is extremely useful for carving and very simple to construct is made by cutting metal banding strips into various lengths and taping the ends of each strip to form a handle. This tool is great for hollowing out arches and tunnels and cutting battlement walls. The hooplike shape makes it ideal for cleaning out large amounts of sand in very little time, something the palette knife can't do. When the band cuts into a vertical plane, the sand falls through the hoop like cheese cut with a wire.

Part of the fun of sandcastling is inventing new tools. Straws, for instance, are a must for sandcastling. They are used for blowing the loose sand away from finished works. But forcing air through a tiny straw can give you an immense headache after a long, hot day. Compressed air in cans (used in the graphic arts trade) works well, but costs money. Our team has been experimenting with a blower made from a large, durable balloon with aquarium tubing and a valve connected to it so the air flow can be regulated.

Cookie cutters make great templates for

(Above) The typically ostentatious plot of the Totally in Sand team. This team has been accused of being a travelling carnival in disguise. *(Opposite)* Carving with palette knives.

46

carving a series of quick reliefs. You can trace around the cutter with a knife and cut away the sand around it. Or the cookie cutter can be sawed in half and hinged with duct tape. This way it can be pressed into the sand pile, quickly carved around, and easily removed by releasing the hinge.

Hollowing out a dome shape or intricate interlocking archways can be done using soft interior forms such as inflatable plastic toys or strong balloons. The soft form is inflated and set inside the constructed wooden form. Sand is mounded around the soft form, and when it is time to carve, the deflated balloon creates a dome shape. This technique takes some practice, but the result is quite satisfactory.

The purpose for all these gadgets and tools is to save time, allowing more detail to be carved. In a four-hour contest, a good hour or two is spent digging and moving sand around. This doesn't leave a lot of time for carving, and ordinarily a contest judge will award points for details. Some contests, however, frown on the use of some of these molds, and it is wise to discuss any questionable techniques beforehand.

Other tools worth mentioning are packing devices. To some groups, their packer is like a mascot: a symbol of the team's pride and experience.

The most popular packers are car axles cut in half. Our group uses a large mallet of hardwood planks bolted together. The packer in the small photo in the beginning of this chapter belongs to the *Orbital Sanders*. Our group, which competes with them, has a love/hate relationship with this instrument. It takes two people to operate, and the *ca-chunga ca-chunga* sound it makes can be heard a quarter mile down the beach. We always know where they are. You can't help loving the ingenuity of it.

Packing devices can be dangerous. They work so well because they are *very* heavy. After five minutes of packing, any sandcastler will swear that the packer weighs a ton. It follows that they can be difficult to maneuver, and can smash the tops of forms if not handled carefully. No one should ever have their hands over the edge of a form when a packer is being used. Having a hand smashed or fingers crushed can drastically shorten an artistic career.

Nelson Zec

(Above) Members of Team Hardcore carving a card from *Alice in Wonderland* at Imperial Beach, California. *(Opposite)* Buckets and shovels at rest after a busy day of sandcastling at Treasure Island, Florida.

— Carving

Artists everywhere, whether they are building sandcastles or painting oil portraits, hear the same refrain: "How do you do that? I can't even draw a straight line." For whatever reason, some people seem compelled to deny that they are "creative." Maybe you are convinced that you lack creative talent. You have had some experience coloring Easter eggs, and you can eat your peanut butter and jelly sandwich down to a remarkable likeness of Santa's sleigh, but that's about it. You think you can do no more.

The truth is, more people suffer from lack of confidence than from lack of talent. Artistic prowess, like any skill, is acquired through dedication and repetition. Very few people are born artistic. Fortunately, sandcastling can be great fun for everyone from professional artists to the most "untalented" soul.

Sculpting is a skill that can be acquired more easily than two-dimensional art forms such as painting and drawing. Principles such as perspective, foreshortening, color, and shadow are not as important in sculpture as they are in art forms that represent three-dimensional figures on a two-dimensional surface. In sand sculpture, the sculptor has to deal with only two key elements: texture (detail) and proportion.

There are basically two types of sand sculptures: animate objects (soft sculpture) and structures (hard sculpture). Animate objects seem to

(Right) Sculpture by Billy Lee of Hawaii. *(Opposite)* Practicing carving skills at White Rock, British Columbia.

51

pose the most problems for beginning sand artists, especially the hands and facial expressions. Beginners tend to add in the details too quickly, before a rough shape is obtained. The results are likely to resemble well-carved pumpkins. Another tendency is concentrating on a known area of comfort and neglecting areas where more experience is needed. You may have mastered eyes and lips, and keep doing them well, but the fingers still look like pickles on all the hands you have done. The entire composition suffers.

Proficiency at anything requires practice. For a sculptor, an objective, well-trained eye creates the piece, not the hands. The eyes must be trained first, before they can tell the hands what to do.

Just for a moment, imagine a cloud bank moving across the sky. You notice a shape, maybe the shape of a dog. Gazing longer, you can make out a particular type of dog: a big, fat wiener dog with short stubby legs. What your eye notices is the outline or contour, a specific shape. Your imagination will fill in more details to give shape to your rotund hound, blocking out shapes that do not fit. Sculpting follows this basic process. Picture a general shape, work down to that shape, and proceed from there.

Now, before you head down to the beach to begin your own "Colossus of Rhodes," settle on an idea of what you want to build. Starting without a goal in mind will simply frustrate you, and your results will be unlikely to draw compliments. Assuming that

Before all the forms are removed, it is necessary to carve away some of the sand to reduce the weight. Darcy Gertz of the Grain Assault team had to work very fast. The tide was only a few feet away by the time he took off the last form.

your fine-art training is limited to stick figures, you might consider working with another medium to learn the basic techniques of sculpting. Clay is a good working medium for practice. It does not behave like sand. The two mediums are entirely different, but the purpose of the practice is to train the eye to compose in three dimensions. Clay has an advantage over other practice mediums like soapstone because it has an elastic quality, allowing one to rework mistakes. It is lighter and easier to transport, as well. Clay is relatively inexpensive, and can be reused if sealed in an airtight container. It will come wrapped in a five-pound brick. You need not purchase any special sculpting tools, but do be sure to find a mess-proof work area.

Without even thinking, stick your hands into the clay and pull off a fistful. It will feel cold, gritty, and slimy. You want to get a feeling for it while you are working it in your hands. If you don't understand the medium you're working with, it will always defeat you. The same applies to sand. Some people may find the feel of clay very unpleasant. I have the same problem with charcoal. Just the thought of working with charcoal sticks on paper makes my teeth grind. If you respond that way to clay, you might try salt dough or something similar.

Roll out a piece of the clay and form a worm. Worms are easy. Looks like a big worm, but could it be a snake? Possibly, but snakes have heads and their tails are tapered.

Totally in Sand

Dragon entryway in progress, and finished sculpture.

Put a head on it by pinching it about two inches from either end. Don't worry about how it looks. The head is the least important part of this piece (it sort of goes along for the ride), but do taper the tail.

Building on this snake idea, let's suppose for a moment that your snake has eaten something so large it can barely slither. Roll out a larger football shape and connect it to the midsection. Now what does it look like? Let your imagination run wild. If you were to add some legs, you might get a sea serpent. But really, can those legs you just imagined support that much weight? If not, maybe they should be made larger.

Now, run your fingers along your creation, smooth it out, and make the repairs. Pinch it in a few places, turn its body and neck this way and that way. Notice how the general shape changes the entire presence of your sculpture with each change in position. Take a few visual snapshots, roll your creation back into its original block shape, and put it away for the day. This last step is to help you avoid a major stumbling block for artists: they get so caught up in congratulating themselves that they don't see the piece objectively. Being able to distinguish between what is worth saving and what should go in the trash is a valuable lesson in art. Too many self-congratulations on a particular piece will hamper your creativity.

So you're done for the day. Your clay is back in its package, and now you are forced to remember what you did while you half-consciously mull over the "what if's"—what you might have done with your clay. This whole process is teaching you to compose in three dimensions.

Tomorrow or the next day, give yourself

Artistic style is something that comes with practice. In the above photo, Bart Frielink of Amsterdam creates a very Gothic cathedral that looks as though it has been around for centuries.

the same amount of time. Believe me, after thinking about it and sleeping on it, you will not only have your snake-serpent idea refined, but chances are this effort will be more realistic and will be completed in less time. Spend more time working in the details, but not before the general shape is roughed in. The detail always comes last.

The eye needs to be trained to notice the components of things, and how they interact to make a good sculpture. Starting with a brick of clay or block of sand can be quite intimidating if you have not had any experience. At least with clay you have the luxury of moving the piece around, something that is not as easy with sand, unless you enjoy digging.

Sculpting tools are merely extensions of your hands and eyes. The fingers and tools glide around the piece. You know it looks right because it feels right, and vice versa. Teach your eyes to glide around the piece without the use of your hands and you will be well on your way to creating some truly fine work.

If there's a compliment in sandcastling that denotes true prestige, it would have to be that he or she is a *carver*. The work of a carver is sure-handed. With something like X-ray vision, the carver can see through a pile of sand to a seductive mermaid or a beautiful fantasy castle. This vision is the sculptor's greatest asset. It is not the peripheral vision that separates the standout running back on a football team, but rather the ability to see the whole of a thing.

A carver notices the components of things. What he sees is not limited to his own

David Henderson

Detail of Bluebeard's Castle. This castle, which stood thirty-seven feet tall from its base, was built by Sand Sculptors International at Treasure Island, Florida.

perspective, but includes other perspectives or facets of an object. This vision results in knowing what the finished piece will look like and what steps it will take to get there.

Carving in the sand is especially difficult, since the composition is often finished from the top down. Other sculpting mediums are composed differently; that is, the sculpting of a piece will normally come together as a whole.

Part of what separates the carver from the stick-figure artist is this understanding of composition. Whereas the stick figure is composed of a circle for a head and lines for the body and appendages, the sculptor sees his piece as something that consists of a skeleton, muscles, tendons, and a personality.

What is probably the most difficult shape to work with, the human figure, follows basic principles of form and proportion in much the same way a building is composed of support beams, windows, and doors. Beginning with the skeleton, the artist has to ask what the bones are doing in a given position, particularly the ones that are not hidden by muscles. Although the skeleton can bend, its elements are inflexible. The hip, elbows, and knees, knuckles, and the heel of the foot, to name a few, are focal points that need to be emphasized. Where bones are hidden by muscles, the form becomes even more difficult, since some muscles are relaxed when others are contracted.

Although the size and shape of the human

A beautiful relief of Native American warriors built by master builder Paul Dawkins of Ottawa, Ontario.

can vary greatly, the rules of composition dictate a uniformity throughout. If the shoulders are made wide, then other body parts should also be made wider.

Whimsical and exaggerated features are popular sand-sculpting themes. Even in whimsy, it is important to know where the features would rest if they weren't made comical. Successful exaggeration requires understanding the fundamentals of proportion.

Since the human face is so difficult to work with, and because mastering the features in it will give you a head start on animal characters, it is a good starting point. The human head is something of an egg shape. Regardless of its position, the eyes will al-

ways fall slightly above the median line that separates the top of the head from the chin. The distance that separates the eyes is the width of an eye. (Imagine a hidden cyclops in your composition.) Eyebrows rest the distance of an eye-width above the eye. The highest point on their arc is approximately one-third their length from the outside point.

The length of the nose is one-fourth the length of the head and begins in the middle of the head. The mouth is one and a half times as wide as the width from nostril to nostril; the lower lip is thicker than the upper.

Begin carving a face by sculpting down to the basic egg shape. The hair, of course, will have to be worked in with this egg shape in mind. Short hair is not a problem. Long

Marc Altamar of Daytona Beach, Florida, recreates a scene from the Bible.

hair requires leaving some sand above and beyond your egg shape.

Since the nose protrudes farthest from the face, it is the first plane to rough-cut. If you extend your hands to form a right angle at the fingertips, you have the angle at which the nose falls back to the face. If you hold your hands in this position on your own face, you will notice that, as well as touching the nose on this plane, it will also (under most circumstances) touch the cheekbone. Where the hands do not rest on the face, the sand will have to be removed.

To sculpt a face, start by marking the reference points on your egg shape. Carve the nose back to the cheek, the dimple between the chin and lower lip, etc. As you carve, keep the relationships in mind.

If you'd like the face to have a little expression, keep these principles in mind. Facial features, including the eyes, mouth, and nose, fall on a horizontal plane when at rest. When in a state of anger or aggression, these horizontal lines tend to come together in the center. Eyebrows point toward the nose; the mouth tightens; and the nostrils flare. Pleasant expressions, on the other hand, are a spreading of these horizontal planes.

The technique of carving varies with each individual. Marc Altamar of Daytona Beach uses only his bare hands for his masterful figures. For large pieces, he has occasionally used his entire body to pack and remove sand. Gerald Lynas of New York City carves with his Frisbee. The disc, he

United Way of Orange County

United Way's "History of Architecture" exhibit at Seal Beach, California. This project required the talents of many master builders and volunteers.

says, is excellent for compressing sand, carving perfect shapes, and, when spun around like an orbital sander, for polishing sand like glass. In Seattle, Charlie Beaulieu has had some forty pieces of laminate cut into every imaginable shape and French curve for his structures.

Carving techniques and tools are a matter of personal preference. You will soon develop your own style of sculpting. Your style will grow with practice and observation. At some point in your experience as a sand sculptor, you will suddenly become aware of your style, and it's that style that will make every sculpture you create unique.

Working in sand presents many sculpting challenges. The art is to turn the sand into something lifelike, whether it be real or imaginary. If you enjoy the work, it will always be reflected in your art.

This sand-sculpted Gulliver makes the bystander look like a life-size Lilliputian.

——— Sandcastling Masters ———

The following is a portfolio of some of the best work that you are likely to see, both on and off the beach. Many of these groups or individuals regard sandcastling as a serious hobby. For others, it has become their livelihood. Almost everyone listed is employed in a creative profession.

Two masters from the Northeast are both artists and have penned books on sandcastling. Michael Di Persio has for the past several years conducted workshops and exhibitions at the Fort Myers Beach contest as well as in his home state of New Jersey. The other, Gerald Lynas of New York City, is a multi-talented artist and Frisbee savant extraordinaire. His film *Sandsong* has earned many prestigious awards, including the 1981 American Film Festival's Blue Ribbon and the CINE Golden Eagle, and was selected by the American Library Association as one of the year's best films.

Florida is home to two master builders. Marc Altamar of Daytona Beach is a professional artist whose interest in sandcastling dates back to his childhood years in Ocean Beach, Maryland. Marc's work is truly masterful. A little farther down the peninsula is the home of Rich Varano, who occupies his

David Watersun

(Above) Detail of a spire by Billy Lee of Hawaii. *(Opposite)* A practice castle, "Star Wars," by the team Sand Sculptors International, preparing for the 1984 world championship at White Rock, British Columbia.

time building castles and sculptures in sand for Sea World in Orlando. Rich also keeps busy organizing contests, no doubt hoping to put Florida on a par with the Pacific Northwest and California as a hub for talent.

In Texas there are those Sons of the Beach, "Amazin' Walter" McDonald and Lucinda "Sandy Feet" Wierenga. This multi-talented duo are the winners of several Texas contests, and their work has been seen in many shopping malls in the South. They are also the authors of a book on sandcastling, and were one-time holders of the world record for the longest sand sculpture, a millipede that snaked some 1.85 miles down the beach at South Padre Island.

In Hawaii, two professional builders, Joe Maize and Billy Lee, can be seen regularly at the Royal Hawaiian in Honolulu and the 505 Front Street Mall in Lahaina, respectively. Joe also competes in contests from time to time on the West Coast, most notably winning the world championship at White Rock in 1983.

Although sandcastling did not originate in Southern California, you would never know it. There is so much talent there, and, of course, they have great weather for the sport. Of the California teams, by far the most famous are the two Sand Sculptors International groups. SSI of San Diego is headed by Gerry Kirk. SSI of Los Angeles is headed by sand guru Todd Vander Pluym and is mentioned in the following chapter. The SSI Los Angeles group goes by the name Team Hardcore in competition.

Gerry Kirk of the SSI of San Diego is a many-time co-world champion and owner of

The Sons of the Beach, "Amazin' Walter" McDonald and Lucinda "Sandy Feet" Wierenga.

several world records. At fifty-six feet, two-inches, his work that appears on page 99 is the present record holder for the tallest castle built with the use of heavy machinery, and was constructed in Kaseda, Japan. Gerry is also the builder of the Maryland state record holder that appears under the Ocean City contest information. The large Garfield was built as a centerpiece for the Fort Lauderdale contest.

An offshoot of the SSI teams are the Arch i Sands headed by Greg LeBon. With eighty percent of their ten-man team employed as architects, it's clear where they got the idea for the team name. The other SSI offshoot is the Sandcastles Unlimited group. Kent Trollen, another architect, heads this group, and was responsible for the History of Architecture portion of the United Way's Seal Beach exhibition in sand.

The only woman to head a Masters team packs plenty of talent. Kali Bradford's California Dreamers were last year's first-place winners at Imperial Beach. Kali is a writer, educator, and artist. For the past six years she has received grants from the California Arts Council through the National Endowment for the Arts.

The San Diego-based Sandyhands is headed by artist and designer Warren Blakely. They tell me that their last sculpture in sand will be their greatest accomplishment: a twelve-hundred-square-foot piece of sandpaper. Papa Zambini (John Danna) tells me that his group, the Great Zambinis, were the first to incorporate paint into their work. Whether or not it was first used by them, they obviously know what they're doing. Look

Todd Vander Pluym of Sand Sculptors International clowning around on Bluebeard's Castle.

for the Zambinis in many contests as well as the annual Christmas exhibition, Santa's Woody, that is constructed each year at Ocean Beach, California.

Gary Kinsella is the last of these sand masters from California. Gary, Norman Kraus, and other key members of SSI groups have put sandcastling on an altogether different plane. Gary's work has been the subject of several magazine articles, television programs, and the Joseph Allen book *Sandcastles*.

It may come as a surprise to some that so many fine teams hail from the Pacific Northwest. Although our wet weather has put the damper on many sandcastling outings, it has also helped to wash a good proportion of silt down from the mountains, giving us excellent sand to work in. With several hundred islands to protect the mainland from pound-

ing surf, the Northwest is home to many of the world's finest sandcastling beaches.

From Seattle come the Orbital Sanders. The perennial Cannon Beach champs have been around for several years. The group is made up mostly of architects, and has an excellent balance of talent. Each year they alternate the captain's chair, so that everyone has a chance to be the top dog.

The other Seattle-based team, Totally In Sand, of which the author is a part, is probably the newest team listed here. They do not, however, lack talent or experience. Charlie Beaulieu has been sandcastling since he was a boy spending summer vacations with his family at Mission Beach. He was also on the world-champion Joe Maize team that took the top honors at White Rock in 1983. Russ Leno, another principal Insander, simply loves carving, whether it be wood, ice, snow, or

Lars Van Nigtevegt of Holland.

sand. His coveted Spam carving trophy is proudly displayed in his house with his other carving awards. Totally In Sand holds the current record for the longest sand sculpture, at 2.979 miles.

British Columbia boasts a multitude of good teams, most notably the Great Sandinis. These one-time world champs have been around for many years and are headed by landscapers Steve Prudente and Doug Harle.

Another great team from British Columbia is headed by Fred Dobbs of the Sandblasters, who likes to build sculptures tall and steep. His 1989 entry at Harrison, B.C., which was built by a very shorthanded team, was the tallest one there at fifteen feet, five inches. It was so impressive that the Guinness folks decided to open a new category for world records: the tallest sandcastle built in one hundred man-hours. Fred and his group helped to top this record just before press time with a new effort at seventeen feet, six inches.

Other builders who participated in this new world record for tallest sandcastle include the Grain Assault team, Artisands des Dreams, and several of the Totally In Sanders from Seattle. The Grain Assault team hails from Vancouver and is headed by jeweler Darcy Gertz. The Artisands are headed by Allan Matsumoto. Both men are avid carvers of sand, ice, and snow. Darcy's pumpkins are well known in the Vancouver area, while Allan's sandcastling team was this year's first-place winner at Harrison. The other Canadian master is Paul Dawkins. His work speaks for itself. Paul is a professional sculptor from Ottawa.

Little did we know that the contest information we requested from Tulsa, Oklahoma, would bring with it a rather vague letter from a gentleman in Holland inquiring about sandcastling activity in the United States. The letter was from a man who is fast becoming one of the author's best sandcastling buddies: Lars Van Nigtevegt of Holland. Lars builds what he likes to call miniature pieces for a miniature country. We were very grateful to be able to include his work. It is unfortunate that we could not include photographs of the work of his mentor, Pieter Wiersma, who recently passed away. It is to be hoped that the litigation stemming from his death will soon be resolved, so that his work can be included in future editions. Pieter was an extraordinary talent.

A future master builder?

Totally In Sand

Artisands Des Dreams

Paul Dawkins

Michael Di Persic

John Danna

John Darna

Jerry Bartlow

Totally In Sand

Fred Dobbs

Rob Cross

Grain Assault

Totally in Sand

Totally In Sand

The Orbital Sanders

Billy Lee

Photographs by G. Augustine Lynas

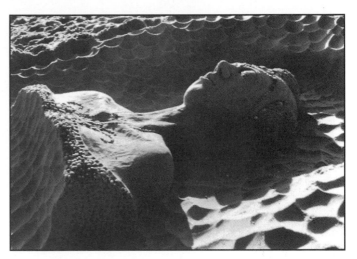

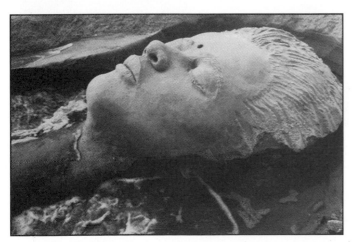

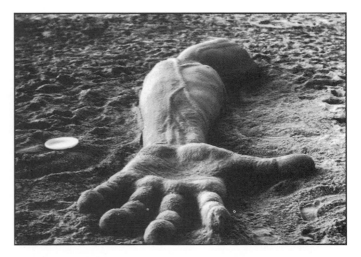

Rob Cross

Totally In Sand

Totally In Sand

Photographs by The Orbital Sanders

Gerry Kirk

News/Sun Sentinel

Gerry Kirk

Kent Trollen

Photographs by United Way of Orange County

Photographs by Walter McDonald

Noel West

Joey Leno

Noel West

Richard Varano

—Setting Up a Contest——

Sandcastle contests are started for a variety of reasons. In Wells, Maine, for instance, the contest began as a demonstration to the local community that the harbor needed to be dredged. It was silted in so badly that sandcastles could be built literally in the middle of it. No matter what prompts its beginning, a sandcastling contest is almost certain to become a popular attraction. The very stealthy city of Carmel, California, now must keep the date of its contest secret until five days prior to the event to insure a truly local contest. On Vancouver Island, the Parksville, B.C., contest has upped its prizes to over $7,000 for the best sculpture, and will draw huge crowds that well justify the rich purse. If there is a single reason why these contests continue to spring up and attract crowds, it would have to be because they are fun: fun to watch, fun to do.

If your beach or community has considered setting up a contest, here are a few suggestions. First and foremost, please have your contest on Saturday. Sandcastling is backbreaking work. It is not unusual for a team to move 35,000 pounds of sand (approximately what a dump truck will hold) and 1200 gallons of water as they build on a twenty-foot-square plot, not to mention packing and carving all that sand while standing

David Henderson

Sandcastling contests can attract tens of thousands. *(Opposite)* The contest at Santa Barbara, California, attracts 50,000 spectators a year, while the contest at White Rock, British Columbia *(above)*, attracted a meager 200,000 a year.

or sitting in all sorts of odd positions. A contest might last only a few hours, but the building, together with the setting up, the tearing down, and the trip home, can make for a long and brutal day. Sandcastlers need a day after the contest before they return to the occupations that support their sandcastling habit.

Competition rules vary as much as the sponsors. There are no national or international standards followed by all contests. Variables include plot size, number of team members, the use of forms, time limits, and, of course, the criteria used by the judges. Some variations are probably for the better, since the beaches themselves vary widely. The real gray area, and biggest problem for both the teams and contest officials, is the judging.

Most sandcastlers would prefer to be judged by their peers. Since this is not always possible, competitions often turn to the next best source: artists, architects, designers, and art teachers. The judging should be based on engineering difficulty, originality, cleverness, sharpness of line, and accuracy of the portrayal. Since sandcastling is a spectator sport, bonus points are sometimes awarded to teams who display the most enthusiasm and are well organized in their plot, but points should not be subtracted for lack of showmanship. Wearing costumes, throwing an occasional bucket of water on rival teams while they're filling their forms, taking ten minutes out for a spot of afternoon tea, or doing a little synchronized swimming all add to the fun of the day. A contest is better judged by a group than by an individual, and the members of the

The annual LEAP contest in San Francisco. LEAP (Learning through Education in the Arts Project) is an organization that provides children in schools access to arts and the opportunity to work side by side with professionals—visual and performing artists and architects. In this photo, LEAP kids team up with Kali Bradford of the California Dreamers.

judging panel should have different backgrounds, if at all possible, to ensure a balanced final opinion. Architects, graphic designers, and art teachers all have slightly different training and perspective for judging "art." An architect might subtract points because the roof tiles do not overlap, for instance, whereas a commercial artist might think the roof is beautiful.

There should be a firm list of criteria of which both the judges and the teams are aware before the contest begins. Last-minute changes in rules should be avoided unless all the teams and judges can be notified. The most objective way to arrive at the winning score is to have each judge award points to each entry. The points can then be tallied like they are in an Olympic event or in an election. In this method, judges should never be

allowed to confer at the end. This helps assure that a particularly vocal judge will not influence his colleagues unduly. Another good idea: include a people's choice award.

Whatever the prizes offered, anybody who participates should be able to go home with a tangible reward—something to show for the event. Buttons, ribbons, and T-shirts are always popular with sandcastlers, and many scrapbooks and refrigerator doors are filled with these souvenirs. These reminders will help motivate the return of participants next year. You may be providing the location, but they are the ones who draw the large crowds to your beach.

The majority of contests take place on an ocean beach and below the high-tide line. In planning for such an event, the organizers should keep the high tide in mind as they

Costumes add to the festivities of a sandcastling contest. Here a team from Houston creates a breakfast entreé for a voracious appetite—"Well Done."

115

choose a starting time. Contests should allow at least three to four hours of actual working time. In several established contests, the actual building time is less than this, but the short time limit automatically limits the scale of the finished entries. With the exception of Masters teams, time limits that exceed four hours will probably overtax the average sandcastler.

Working below the high-tide line saves the builders time in carrying water to their plot, since the sand is wet and the water table is usually no more than a shovelful down. However, contests need not be held where the sculptures will wash away at the end of the day. A contest held above the high-tide line will allow the pieces to stand several days (sandcastles can stand a remarkably long time if they are packed well and sprayed

with binders that prevent evaporation); they will continue to attract people to the beach long after the teams have gone home. It's a good idea to have someone keep an eye on the site if you want to keep the sculptures intact for a while. If you do decide to have your contest above the high-tide line, be sure to allow time for carrying water in the actual building time.

Plot sizes vary with each contest and category. For a Masters division, a thirty-foot-square plot is almost standard for eight-member teams, while forty by forty feet is more common for ten-member teams. The average size for the adult novice category is twenty by twenty feet; pairs and solo castlers usually work in a slightly smaller plot.

There are two basic ways to lay out plots. Either contest sponsors can stake them out,

Competitive sandcastles and sculptures should be judged on originality, engineering difficulty, sharpness of line, use of space, and accuracy of portrayal. In some instances bonus points are awarded to the teams that display the most enthusiasm and are the most organized.

or they can give each team four stakes and an appropriate length of rope. If the officials stake out plots, they can dictate what division works where, and can spread the teams out to prevent a crowd bottleneck. (Masters teams prefer to castle close together, to draw the spectators and the judges to one area.) If your contest site is below the high-tide line, plot stakes must be placed quickly so the competition can start and end on time. Otherwise, that really big wave can roll in and ruin a lot of pieces before they are even completed.

Eight- and ten-member sandcastling teams are common in competition, but a good team does not have to be that large. In fact, smaller teams of four or six should be encouraged. It is nearly impossible to keep a team of eight or ten together for an entire summer of sandcastling. A smaller team greatly reduces the amount of equipment to be hauled and the expense of travelling. Smaller groups may have to scale down the size of their work, but the quality can remain just as high. Children can be allowed to participate both in their own division and with adults. Children's categories, however, should not include any adult participation, except in the form of limited advice.

Sandcastling is usually a community-participation event since permission to use the beach is required. Attracting teams to your beach need not be difficult if you organize well. Don't plan your event around a large number of master teams; there simply aren't that many serious teams around. Other categories can easily be filled if the contest is

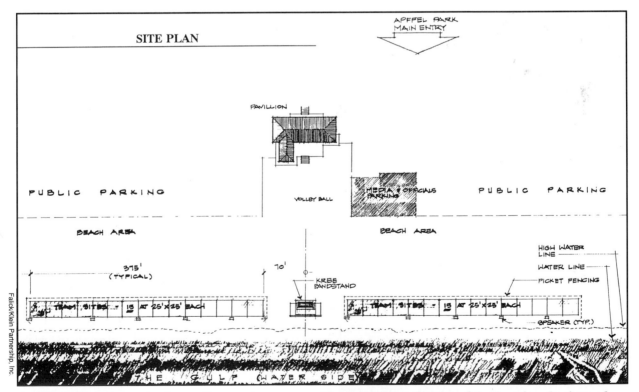

A sandcastling contest site layout for a contest sponsored by the Houston Chapter of the American Institute of Architects. The total layout design should be well thought out as in this illustration—a judges' walkway, parking facilities, speaker boxes, and, of course, the actual sandcastling plots.

planned and publicized well in advance. Special high-school and college-age categories can attract some strong rivals. Local businesses, architectural firms, and other creative professions can also form strongly competitive groups. Family categories are popular, too, and children should always be encouraged to participate.

A well-managed sandcastling event can grow to attract tens of thousands of spectators to your beach. Parking can be an immense problem; so can controlling litter and alcohol consumption. Careful planning in these areas can avert many unpleasant experiences for both visitors and participants. Portable bathrooms and extra litter barrels,

for instance, are highly recommended if you're expecting a big crowd. Many beaches that do not normally allow parking on the beach sometimes bend their rules, allowing teams to drive to their plots to unload their equipment.

If your beach is in a remote location or sandcastling is something new to your area, you might consider inviting a professional team to judge your contest, conduct workshops, and build an exhibition. In communities where the beach is rather small, a full-blown competition can be completed in heats, with a final championship at the end of the summer.

Where beach access is difficult, you might consider limiting your contest. As long as the rules are specifically explained, limitations should not discourage entries. Most contests allow forms to be used in the initial construction; however, sandcastling forms are heavy and difficult to transport. Prohibiting the use of forms is unlikely to keep entrants away.

Another tactic to consider: most of the teams we've contacted agree that an improvisational contest (one in which the theme is picked right before the starting time) can be very attractive, since it saves them time and money they would otherwise spend on practicing. Improvisation gives the purists a chance to show off, too. Of course, there's nothing wrong in having more than one contest per summer; several beaches do.

As for smaller communities that are just starting contests, you can't expect an influx of teams and spectators in the first year.

Marvin Guillermo

Winner of the "Mother and Son" category at the contest in Carmel, California.

Extending personal invitations to specific groups or teams will help boost the turnout. Offering a large purse will increase the attraction for serious builders. However, many successful contests offer little or no cash incentives. The more important thing is to get the teams and spectators involved through advertising during the first few years. The cash prize can always be increased after the contest is well established.

At some beaches, the sandcastle contest is the biggest attraction of the summer. It can take some time for a contest to gain that kind of momentum. Before launching it as a solo event, you might want to consider merging your contest with another established beach event to provide more exposure. An example would be to have the sandcastle contest dur-ing a kite festival. Kite-flying and sandcastling are a marriage made in heaven. The sandcastling keeps the spectators on the beach when the winds are down, and when the winds are up, heads can turn in every direction, taking in all the activities, and making it a very satisfying day. Many of your visitors will probably return to your beach even when nothing in particular is going on.

Not all the contests listed in this book are sponsored by the chambers of commerce or community recreation departments. Several private and corporate organizations are getting involved, since there is good publicity in supporting contests of this nature. The American Institute of Architects sponsors approximately one out of every five contests. Contact the chapter in your area for their

A young girl creates a *Ghostbusters* ghoul in Atlantic City, New Jersey.

advice and support. Any community planning to start a contest should be aware that once a contest becomes established, it is very difficult to slow its growth. Some contests begin to have serious problems with congestion within a few years; be sure to plan for managing future crowds and traffic even in the first year of your competition.

The general rule of thumb regarding what may occur inside the plot is that sculptures may consist of sand from the plot only and water from the ocean or lake. Nothing that pollutes or is unnatural may be used. The gray area is always what constitutes "unnatural." If you're going to allow sea shells, water-based paint, dry ice, and flowers to be used, it should be specifically spelled out in the rules. A captains' meeting should be held before the contest, and any questions regarding rules and regulations should be addressed then.

Many competitions have no categories; the contest is open. Have as many categories as you can successfully fill. This will allow more groups to place in the judging. There could be adult novice, family, special group, small team, and youth categories. There should also be a Master's category, which includes previous contest winners and seasoned veterans. The plot size should reflect the level of expertise of each category. Children should be allowed to receive limited advice from their parents or guardians.

Sandcastling contests can even be held at a spot where there is no beach. It might be a shopping mall, a parking lot, or on the steps of the city hall, like the AIA-sponsored contest in Palo Alto, California. In these circumstances, the sand is trucked in for the competition. In choosing an off-the-beach location, remember that the sand-water mixture needs to drain, and keep in mind the amount of weight involved. A parking lot surface may not provide adequate drainage, and since there is a tendency to over-water, the base could become so saturated that the whole thing would collapse. For whatever reason you may decide to launch a contest, with some good planning and a little hard work it should be successful. Many of the contest organizers listed in this book will gladly help you get your contest started.

(Below) A very steep pyramid built in San Francisco, California. *(Opposite)* The Cabrillo Marine Museum Contest in San Pedro, California, requires that the builders incorporate themselves into the sculptures.

Bob Walker

121

Not all sandcastling events are contests. Many, like the Alice in Wonderland sculpture at the Santa Monica Place mall, are built strictly for exhibition, to give audiences a chance to enjoy sandcastling as an art. The Alice in Wonderland exhibition required 170 tons of sand and stood for several months before it was replaced by another sand sculpture. The builders, Todd Vander Pluym and the Sand Sculptors International group of Los Angeles, worked on the project for hundreds of hours. Other sandcastling events are a sort of hybrid between competition and exhibition: world record attempts. These efforts can require even more planning and expense than a full-fledged contest.

If there is an exception to our earlier statement that sandcastling teams rarely have "stars," it would have to be Todd Vander Pluym. His sculptures have been seen and admired on every continent except Antarctica. Todd is the winner of hundreds of competitions, organizer of several world-record events, and builder of exhibitions in almost every developed country. Todd is the closest thing to a guru in sandcastling today. Together with his Sand Sculptors International team, Todd has been an ambassador for sandcastling, opening doors for the immense potential of this relatively new art form. Any sandcastling team would consider it the highlight of their career to dethrone Todd at the U.S. Open, where his string of championships is still unbroken.

David Henderson

(Above and Opposite) This "Alice in Wonderland" exhibition, built by Todd Vander Pluym and Sand Sculptors International, required 170 tons of sand and stood for several months before it was torn down and replaced by another sand sculpture.

Given the crisp detail and durability of some of the sculptures illustrated in this chapter, you might wonder if sand is the only medium used in some of the work. Like many building materials, sand can be ranked as to grade. The purest ocean beach sand is often too clean to be used in world-record or exhibition sculptures. Once the moisture evaporates from this sand, the structures collapse. But other types of sand, particularly sand that comes from quarries, actually get stronger as they dry out. Like cement, sand like this can dry rock hard, and yet will crumble in your hands with enough pressure. Sandcastlers hunt for sand with this quality for special projects.

World records for sandcastling fall into several categories. The Guinness Book of World Records lists the tallest (with the use of heavy machinery) at fifty-six feet, two inches; it was built in Kaseda, Japan, in 1989 by Gerry Kirk and the SSI team based in San Diego. The planning, expense, and time required to create one of these huge sandcastles are illustrated well in the accompanying photographs of Bluebeard's Castle, which was constructed at Treasure Island, Florida. The thirty-seven-foot-high gem required some 17,000 tons of sand and was built with the help of several hundred volunteers and professional builders.

The second category of world record

A sandcastle built by Paul Dawkins of Ottawa, Ontario. This sculpture, designed for display in a mall, is a daring example of pushing the cohesiveness of sand to its limit.

124

recognized by Guinness is the longest sandcastle. Competition for this record has turned into an all-out war between two cities: Myrtle Beach, South Carolina, and Long Beach, Washington. For instance, the Myrtle Beach record of 2.85 miles was set in early June, 1989, by some 2,000 builders with the help of Marc Altamar and Todd Vander Pluym's team. That record stood for a mere six weeks before the Totally in Sand group, with about four hundred volunteers, exceeded that length by some six hundred feet at Long Beach. At press time, the two beaches planned to compete for the coveted record on the same weekend in 1990. These world-record sculptures are a true test of endurance for the builders. With the exception of the centerpiece, the work is completed and washed away by the tide in less than a day. It will not be surprising if South Padre Island, Texas, soon becomes involved in this cross-coast rivalry. South Padre Island's 1.85-mile-long "Millipede" was once the record holder, and the Sons of the Beach and their friends from the Lone Star State are not likely to let the current war go very far before they put their hand in once again.

Another record category recently opened by the Guinness Book is the tallest sandcastle built in a hundred man-hours. The use of heavy machinery is not allowed in this category. As of press time, that record stands

One of five Japanese fairy tales exhibited in sand. "The Crab and the Monkey" was built by Todd Vander Pluym and Sand Sculptors International in Nygoya, Japan.

at seventeen feet, six inches, established by Pacific Northwest Sand Shapers, a coalition of four teams from Washington state and British Columbia, at Harrison Hot Springs, British Columbia. The Southern California groups probably will not allow this record to stand for long. New records are likely to run very quickly into the low twenties, and then increase by inches rather than feet as builders push the limits of their medium.

Exhibitors constructing indoor castles and sculptures have to contend with special challenges beyond enthusiasm, creativity, and the quality of the sand. Drainage can be problem for sandcastling indoors, where floors do not absorb excess moisture. Tons of sand sculpture can literally hydroplane along the surface of an oversaturated base. Outdoors or indoors, there seems to be a fourteen-foot height barrier that is difficult to surmount. Building higher requires great care in packing and proper design in forms used. Despite the difficulties, we can rest assured that records will continue to be shattered and exhibitions will continue to grow more elaborate. Even as the sport gains popularity in Europe, Japan, Australia, and New Zealand, rivalries continue to heat up in the established centers of sandcastling, and techniques grow more sophisticated by the day. Who knows what the future holds for sandcastling?

(Above) "Sleeping Beauty's Castle"—another epic sand sculpture—built by Sand Sculptors International, has been featured in many magazines. *(Opposite)* Dave Henderson puts the finishing touches on this Super Bowl exhibit in San Diego, California.

(Above) More details from the "Alice in Wonderland" exhibit at the Santa Monica Place mall in Santa Monica, California. *(Opposite)* Detail of an indoor sand sculpture over twenty feet in height.

Photographs by David Henderson

Photographs by David Henderson

(Above and Opposite) This sandcastle built in Kamaishi, Japan, by Todd Vander Pluym and Sand Sculptors International, towered over thirty feet in height. *(Pages 132-133)* Sandcastle exhibition built at Sundland Park Mall in El Paso, Texas, by the Sons of the Beach.

Photographs by David Henderson

The making of a world record: Bluebeard's Castle in progress as it appeared from ground level. The sculpture would top some thirty-seven feet and would require 17,000 tons of sand.

(Above and following two pages) The building of an exhibition of the magnitude of Bluebeard's Castle requires good organization. The hours spent by all involved in the project ran into thousands. Many professionals as well as volunteers joined together to put on a show of shows for sandcastling.

An attempt to build a twenty-two foot indoor castle for the Seattle Boat Show in the Kingdome.

Gerry Kirk

The Contests

To assemble the following list of North American sandcastling competitions, over three hundred letters were sent to chambers of commerce and community recreation departments. We discovered some of the contests not through official channels, but by word of mouth or by stroke of luck. In all, information on more than ninety contests is assembled on the following pages.

How many contests actually take place each year is difficult to say. One magazine estimated the number of contests in the United States at about eight hundred. We think this figure may be high, but there are undoubtedly more contests than the ones listed here. If your community hosts an annual contest that is not listed in this book, let us know. We will gladly include it in future editions.

Don't be surprised if the dates change for some of these contests. Many contest dates are set with the extreme low tide in mind. In some cases, the contest scheduling moves around so much that we've listed the approximate time of year that the contest is held, or a "target weekend" (such as the third Saturday in July, for instance), rather than citing specific dates. If you plan to attend a contest, either to participate or to observe, be sure to contact the organizer of the contest well ahead of time.

Totally in Sand

Date: Fourth of July

Sponsor: South East Chapter of the American Institute of Architects

Plot Size: 20' x 20'

Time Allowed: 4 hours

Entry Fee: None

Prizes: Yes (see Comments)

Age Categories: Youth and Adult

Competition Categories: Open

Comments: The Juneau contest is held at Sandy Beach, and there is no limit to the number of contestants that may enter. In past years, winners have been flown to the Imperial Beach Contest compliments of Alaska Airlines.

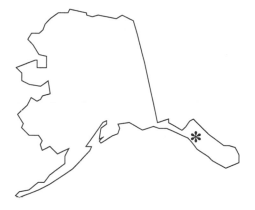

For More Information:

Sandcastling Contest
Cathy Fritz
City Engineering Dept.
155 South Seward St.
Juneau, AK 99801

Noel West

Parksville, British Columbia

Date: Mid July

Sponsor: City of Parksville

Plot Size: Varies with level

Time Allowed: 4 hours

Entry Fee: Yes

Prizes: Cash awards; First Place in Masters category, $7,000+

Age Categories: Youth and Adult

Competition Categories: Masters, Novice, Executive Sandbox, Youth, and Man and His Toys

Comments: The B.C. Open Sandcastle Competition is one of the richest purses in sandcastling. Expect teams from Hawaii, California, and Washington to compete with the Canadians in this very competitive contest. Over $20,000 in prize money is available in 1990. $2,500 is allotted to the children's category alone. This contest has picked up where the White Rock Contest left off.

For More Information:

The B.C. Open
P.O. Box 1769
Parksville, BC V0R 2S0
Canada

The Orbital Sanders

·Harrison Hot Springs, British Columbia·

Date: Early September

Sponsor: Harrison Hot Springs Sand Sculpture Society

Plot Size: Master, 45' x 45'; other categories are open

Time Allowed: Masters, 2 days, 5 hours each day; other categories, 3-4 hours.

Entry Fee: Yes

Prizes: Cash awards ($5,000 for winner in Masters category) and ribbons

Age Categories: Youth and Adult

Competition Categories: Several

Comments: The contest at Harrison Hot Springs offers one of the best Masters competitions in North America. The sand at Harrison Hot Springs is some of the best sand in the world to build with. Not one sculpture has ever collapsed during a contest held here, and many of the sculptures are over 15 feet high with very small bases. Watch for this contest to become recognized as a world sandcastling event.

For More Information:

Harrison Hot Springs
World Championship Sand
Sculpture
P.O. Box 266
Harrison Hot Springs, BC
V0M 1K0 Canada

Fred Dobbs

Penticton, British Columbia

Date: Last Thursday of July

Sponsor: Leisure Services Department and The Penticton Knights

Plot Size: 15' x 15'

Time Allowed: 2.5 hours

Entry Fee: Yes

Prizes: Cash and trophies

Age Categories: Youth and Adult

Competition Categories: Four

Comments: The Penticton contest is the only evening contest, and one of the few that do not take place on a weekend. The weather is usually very warm in late July in Penticton, making for a pleasant evening of sandcastling.

For More Information:

Sandcastling Contest/
Peach Festival
City of Penticton
325 Power Street
Penticton, BC V2A 7K9
Canada

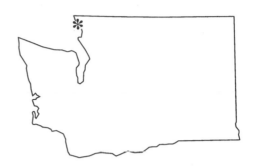

Date: Three contests in June, July, and August
Sponsor: Birch Bay Chamber of Commerce
Plot Size: Open
Time Allowed: Under 4 hours
Entry Fee: None
Prizes: Trophies and awards
Age Categories: Youth and Adult
Competition Categories: Open
Comments: The Birch Bay Chamber of Commerce hosts a number of family-oriented sandcastling contests throughout the summer. The sand is excellent for constructing castles and sculptures. Expect more serious builders to enter these contests as practice for the larger British Columbia competitions.

For More Information:

Sandcastling Contest
Pat Alesse
4895 Birch Bay Lynden Rd.
Birch Bay, WA 98230

Fred Dobbs

Port Townsend, Washington

Date: Third week in July

Sponsor: The Sand Castle toy store

Plot Size: Open

Time Allowed: 5 hours

Entry Fee: None

Prizes: Yes

Age Categories: Youth and Adult

Competition Categories: Several

Comments: The Port Townsend Sandcastle Contest is held at nearby Fort Worden. This regional contest has grown steadily in popularity, and will continue to grow as more teams become aware of it.

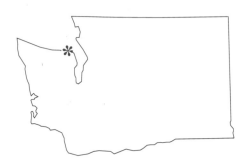

For More Information:

Sandcastling Contest
The Sand Castle
840 Water Street
Port Townsend, WA 98368

Totally In Sand

Everett, Washington

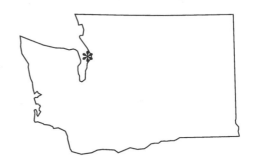

Date: Mid-June to mid-July

Sponsor: Everett Parks & Recreation Department

Plot Size: 20' x 20'

Time Allowed: Under 4 hours

Entry Fee: None

Prizes: Awards

Age Categories: Youth and Adult

Competition Categories: Open

Comments: The Everett Sandcastle Contest is held in conjunction with the Everett Jetty Days. Contestants must take a small ferry out to the jetty where the contest is held. Contestants should plan to take only as many tools as they can carry in one trip.

For More Information:

Sandcastling Contest
Jane Lewis
Everett Parks & Recreation Department
3002 Wetmore Avenue
Everett, WA 98201

Artisards Des Dreams

147

Seattle, Washington

Date: Early August

Sponsor: The Keg Restaurant, KPLZ, and KVI Radio

Plot Size: 20' x 15'

Time Allowed: 4 hours

Entry Fee: Yes

Prizes: Cash awards and prizes

Age Categories: Youth and Adult

Competition Categories: Sandcastles, Sea Creatures, and Family Fun

Comments: The Keg Sand Blast is held the weekend after the Seattle Seafair Hydroplane Races. Although past contests have been held at Alki Beach in West Seattle, the sponsors might be moving the contest to another beach in the Seattle area in order to accommodate larger crowds. Advance registration is recommended.

For More Information:

Keg Sand Blast
Hope Pettinger,
Marketing Director
14655 Belred Rd., Suite 102
Bellevue, WA 98007

Copalis, Washington

Date: Labor Day weekend

Sponsor: Washington Coast Chamber of Commerce

Plot Size: 20' x 20'

Time Allowed: 4 hours

Entry Fee: Yes

Prizes: Trophies and awards

Age Categories: Youth and Adult

Competition Categories: Open

Comments: The sandcastling contest in Copalis Beach was originally held on the Fourth of July, but is now held Labor Day weekend. Expect this contest to grow in future years.

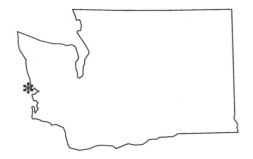

For More Information:

Sandcastling Contest
Washington Coast
Chamber of Commerce
P.O. Box 562
Copalis Beach, WA 98563

Richard Varano

Long Beach, Washington

Date: Mid to late July
Sponsor: City of Long Beach
Plot Size: 20' x 20'
Time Allowed: 4 hours
Entry Fee: Yes
Prizes: Cash awards and prizes
Age Categories: Youth and Adult
Competition Categories: Open Class, Masters, Novice, Youth, and Family
Comments: The Long Beach Sandsations Contest continues to up its purse each year. Cash prizes totalling $3,000 are available in 1990. In addition to the annual Sandsations Contest, the City of Long Beach hosts an annual attempt to break the world record for the longest sand sculpture. Volunteers are welcome in this effort to hold Long Beach's title against Myrtle Beach, South Carolina. Long Beach is the current record holder at 2.979 miles.

For More Information:

Sandsations
P.O. Box 562
Long Beach, WA 98631

Vicki Morgan

———— Cannon Beach, Oregon ————

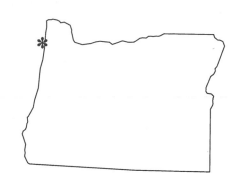

Date: Early May, depending on tide schedule

Sponsor: Cannon Beach Chamber of Commerce

Plot Size: 20' x 20'

Time Allowed: 4 hours

Entry Fee: $8.00 per team member (up to 8 per team)

Prizes: Art in Sand Award, Best Sandcastle, and other awards

Age Categories: Several youth and adult

Competition Categories: Open

Comments: Sandcastle Day at Cannon Beach is one of the premier contests. Attendance figures often surpass 30,000, making this tiny Oregon beach a bit crowded. Both contestants and spectators, however, seem to love and thrive on the number of people that show up each year. A Masters category has been added for 1990. Advance registration is recommended.

For More Information:

Sandcastle Day
Cannon Beach
Chamber of Commerce
P.O. Box 64
Cannon Beach, OR 97110

The Orbital Sanders

Rockaway Beach, Oregon

Date: Late September / early October

Sponsor: Rockaway Beach Chamber of Commerce

Plot Size: 20' x 20'

Time Allowed: 4 hours

Entry Fee: Yes

Prizes: Cash awards and prizes

Age Categories: Youth and Adult

Competition Categories: Open Class, Family, and Youth

Comments: One of the last sandcastling contests to be held each year on the West Coast, the Rockaway contest is held in conjunction with the Autumn Festival, which includes many other beach-related activities.

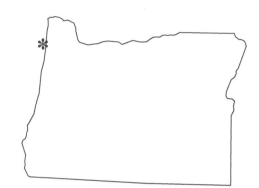

For More Information:

Sandcastle Contest
Rockaway Beach
Chamber of Commerce
P.O. Box 190
Rockaway, OR 97136

Totally in Sand

Date: Mid-August

Sponsor: Lincoln City Parks & Recreation Department and Lincoln City Chamber of Commerce

Plot Size: 20' x 20'

Time Allowed: 2 hours

Entry Fee: None

Prizes: Trophies and awards

Age Categories: Youth and Adult

Competition Categories: Open

Comments: The family-oriented Lincoln City Sandcastle Contest has been established for more than a decade and a half. Lincoln City Beach, like many Oregon beaches, is simply breathtaking. A great contest for the novice builder.

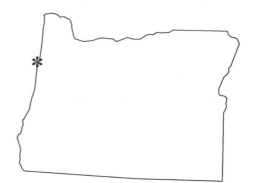

For More Information:

Sandcastle Contest
2150 NE Oar Place
Lincoln City, OR 97367

Western World

Bandon, Oregon

Date: Memorial Day

Sponsor: Bandon Chamber of Commerce and Lions Club

Plot Size: 20' x 20'

Time Allowed: 5 hours

Entry Fee: Yes

Prizes: Small cash awards and ribbons

Age Categories: Several Youth and Adult

Competition Categories: Open

Comments: This small Oregon city offers an excellent sandcastling contest and manages each year to have a great turnout. This is an excellent contest for families and novice builders.

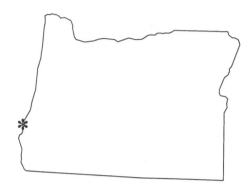

For More Information:

Sandcastling Contest
Bandon Chamber
of Commerce
P.O. Box 1515
Bandon, OR 97411

Western World

Date: Saturday following the Fourth of July weekend
Sponsor: Kootenai County Centennial Committee and KZZU Radio
Plot Size: 10' x 10'
Time Allowed: 3-4 hours
Entry Fee: None
Prizes: Yes (see Comments)
Age Categories: Youth and Adult
Competition Categories: Open Pairs
Comments: Lake Coeur d'Alene is considered one of the most beautiful lakes in the world. The sand at Lake Coeur d'Alene, however, is more difficult to build with than the sand at many other beaches, and challenges contestants both artistically and structurally. A nice incentive for entering this contest: for the past two years, Alaska Airlines has offered the top four winning pairs free airfare to San Diego, California, to compete in the U. S. Open Sandcastle Contest as a team.

For More Information:

Sandcastling Contest
Kootenai County
Centennial Committee
c/o Mary Waggoner
P. O. Box 1210
Hayden Lake, ID 83835

Coeur d'Alene Chamber of Commerce

Date: September

Sponsor: LEAP (Learning through Education in the Arts Project)

Plot Size: 20' x 20'

Time Allowed: 5 hours

Entry Fee: Yes

Prizes: Awards and trophies

Special Rules: Two young people must participate in the building of structure

Age Categories: Adult with youth participation

Competition Categories: Several

Comments: Please note that the LEAP Sandcastle Contest requires that two youths play an integral part in the building of each team's entry. The contest is open to all design-related professions and firms. It is held at San Francisco's Aquatic Park.

For More Information:

The LEAP
Sandcastle Contest
1409 Bush Street
San Francisco, CA 94109

Date: Early June

Sponsor: Alameda Parks & Recreation Dept.

Plot Size: Open

Time Allowed: 3 hours

Entry Fee: None

Prizes: Trophies and ribbons

Age Categories: Youth and Adult

Competition Categories: Sandcastle/Sand-sculpture

Comments: Established in 1964, the Alameda Sandcastle Contest is held at Robert W. Crown Memorial State Beach. Because of its reputation as the granddaddy of sand-castling contests, advance registration is recommended.

For More Information:

Sandcastle Contest
Alameda Parks &
Recreation Department
City Hall
Santa Clara Ave. & Oak St.
Alameda, CA 94501

Alameda Parks and Recreation Dept.

Date: Late June

Sponsor: Santa Clara Valley Chapter of the American Institute of Architects, and the City of Palo Alto

Plot Size: 8' x 8'

Time Allowed: 2 hours

Entry Fee: $50.00

Prizes: Best of Show, Best Theme, Best Historical Replica, Best Fantasy Castle

Age Categories: Adult

Competition Categories: Several themes

Comments: The Palo Alto contest is unique in that sand for the castling is trucked into the plaza at the foot of City Hall. Because space is limited, advance registration is recommended.

For More Information:

Sandcastle Contest
Katherine Davis
36 South 1st St., Suite 200
San Jose, CA 95113

Grain Assault

Capitola, California

Date: Labor Day Weekend
Sponsor: Capitola Begonia Festival
Plot Size: 20' x 20'
Time Allowed: 4 hours
Entry Fee: None
Prizes: Trophies and awards
Age Categories: Youth and Adult
Competition Categories: Open
Comments: Because there is no limit to the number of builders in a plot, it is common to have teams of 20 to 30 builders in this competition.

For More Information:

Sandcastle Contest
Begonia Festival
P.O. Box 501
Capitola, CA 95010

Larry Davis

Carmel, California

Date: Date kept secret until five days prior to event, but reliable sources confirm that it generally takes place between September and November

Sponsor: Monterey Bay Chapter of the American Institute of Architects

Plot Size: 20' x 20'

Time Allowed: 4 hours

Entry Fee: None

Prizes: Awards and trophies

Age Categories: Youth and Adult; Mother and Son category

Competition Categories: Theme is picked for each year

Comments: Established in 1962, the Carmel Sandcastle Contest has had quite an illustrious past. The current Grand Sand Marshall, Marvin Guillermo (a reliable source), did confirm that everyone is encouraged to bribe the judges with food and drink as well as other tokens of affection. Such bribes, however, in no way affect the judge's decision.

For More Information:

Sandcastle Contest
Monterey Bay Chapter AIA
200 San Benancio Road
Salinas, CA 93908

Marvin Guillermo

Fresno, California

Date: Late August

Sponsor: Fresno Chapter of the American Institute of Architects

Plot Size: 20' x 20'

Time Allowed: 4 hours

Entry Fee: Yes

Prizes: Trophies and awards

Age Categories: Adult

Competition Categories: Open

Comments: This inland sandcastle contest, which is held at Millerton Lake, serves two purposes: (1) every year the sand hauled in for the contest helps rebuild the beach at the lake, and (2) the contest provides a fun time for all who participate. Each year additional categories have been created for the contest to accomodate the continued growth.

For More Information:

Sandcastle Contest
Fresno Chapter A.I.A
Skip Carlstrom
1589 West Shaw, Suite101
Fresno, CA 93711

H.S. Barsam

Pismo Beach, California

Date: Late October

Sponsor: Pismo Beach Clam Festival and the Pismo Beach Parks and Recreation Dept.

Plot Size: 20' x 20'

Time Allowed: 4 hours

Entry Fee: None

Prizes: Cash prizes

Age Categories: Youth and Adult

Competition Categories: Open

Comments: The community of Pismo Beach hosts several sandcastle contests throughout the summer, ending with the last contest held during the Clam Festival. Because this is the final sandcastling event of the year at Pismo Beach, advance registration is recommended.

For More Information:

Sandcastle Contest
Pismo Beach
Chamber of Commerce
581 Dolliver Street
Pismo Beach, CA 93449

The Orbital Sanders

Date: Third Saturday in August

Sponsor: Grover City Recreation Department

Plot Size: Open

Time Allowed: 2.5 hours

Entry Fee: None

Prizes: Awards donated by local merchants

Age Categories: Youth and Adult

Competition Categories: Open

Comments: The sandcastle contest is part of the Grover City Beach Party and is held at Pismo State Beach. This beach is popular not only for sandcastling, but also for its dunes. Expect to see lots of dune buggies.

For More Information:

Sandcastle Contest
Grover City Recreation Dept.
P.O. Box 365
Grover City, CA 93433

Date: September

Sponsor: Santa Barbara City Recreation Dept. and the Santa Barbara Bank & Trust

Plot Size: 15' x 15'

Time Allowed: 3 hours

Entry Fee: Yes

Prizes: $4,000 in cash awards available

Age Categories: Youth and Adult

Competition Categories: Sandcastle and Sand-sculpture

Comments: Expect a large turnout for this popular contest, which has a history of strong support from the city of Santa Barbara. The prize money donated by the Santa Barbara Bank & Trust goes to the winner's favorite non-profit organization.

For More Information:

Sandcastle Contest
Santa Barbara
Recreation Department
Aquatics Division
P.O. Drawer P-P
Santa Barbara, CA 93102

Larry Davis

Ventura, California

Date: Last weekend in April

Sponsor: Ventura Recreation Department

Plot Size: 20' x 20'

Time Allowed: 4 hours

Entry Fee: None

Prizes: Trophies

Age Categories: Groups—no limit

Competition Categories: Sandcastles and Free Form

Comments: The Ventura contest is part of the two-day California Beach Party held every last weekend in April. The city of Ventura hosts other contests, but this sandcastling contest is known as the "big one."

For More Information:

Sandcastle Contest
Special Events
P.O. Box 99
Ventura, CA 93002

Paul Dawkins

Date: Sunday of the first full weekend in October

Sponsor: City of Port Hueneme

Plot Size: 20' x 20'

Time Allowed: 4 hours

Entry Fee: None

Prizes: Cash prizes

Age Categories: Youth and Adult

Competition Categories: Open

Comments: Each year the Port Hueneme Sandcastle Contest attracts a good crowd. Children are encouraged to build individually or as part of a team that includes adults. A fine family-oriented contest.

For More Information:

Sandcastle Contest
Penny Wolcott
646 Bard Road
Port Hueneme, CA 93041

Joey Leno

Santa Monica, California

Date: Early August

Sponsor: Los Angeles Chapter of the American Institute of Architects and USG Interiors

Plot Size: Open

Time Allowed: 6 hours

Entry Fee: Yes; proceeds from the entry fees go to a scholarship fund

Prizes: Trophies and awards

Age Categories: Adult and Children Under 10 Years of Age

Competition Categories: Sandcastle and Sand-sculpture—both individuals and teams; an Anything Goes category for children under 10 years of age

Comments: Entries are limited to twenty-four teams. The public is encouraged to join with the team of an architectural firm or to build individually.

For More Information:

Sandcastle Competition
c/o Andrew Althaus
3780 Wilshire Blvd. Ste. 900
Los Angeles, CA 90010

Warren Blakely

Date: First Sunday in August

Sponsor: Long Beach Chamber of Commerce

Plot Size: 20' x 20'

Time Allowed: 4 hours

Entry Fee: Yes

Prizes: Trophies

Age Categories: Youth and Adult

Competition Categories: Several

Comments: This southern California contest, now in its twenty-fourth year, always attracts large crowds. Advance registration is recommended.

For More Information:

Sandcastle Contest
Long Beach Area
Chamber of Commerce
P.O. Box 690
Long Beach, CA 90801

Warren Blakely

Date: Mid to late October

Sponsor: Cabrillo Marine Museum

Plot Size: Open

Time Allowed: 3 hours

Entry Fee: None

Prizes: Awards, ribbons, and trophies

Age Categories: 13 Years Old and Younger;
14 Years Old and Up

Competition Categories: One

Comments: This "Living Sand Sculpture Contest" is one of a kind. Its rules specify that all contestants must in some way incorporate *themselves* into their sand sculpture—regardless of their age. A great contest for children and families.

For More Information:

Living Sand
Sculpture Contest
Cabrillo Marine Museum
3720 Stephen White Drive
San Pedro, CA 90731

Cabrillo Marine Museum

Date: Early to mid September

Sponsor: United Way

Plot Size: 20' x 20'

Time Allowed: 4 hours

Entry Fee: Corporations, $50.00; agencies, $25.00

Prizes: Trophies

Age Categories: Youth and Adult

Competition Categories: Sandcastle and Sand Sculpture

Comments: This six-year-old contest serves as a kick-off for the region's United Way drive. Pictured below is a detail from the United Way's History of Architecture, a special sandsculpture project built on Seal Beach in 1987. The sculpture was executed by the Sandcastles Unlimited group headed by Ken Trollen, with the assistance of many professional builders and volunteers.

For More Information:

United Way
Sandcastle Event
P. O. Box 8130
Orange, CA 92664

United Way of Orange County

170

Date: Mid to late September

Sponsor: The Newport Beach Chamber of Commerce and The Commodores Club

Plot Size: 15' x 15'

Time Allowed: 3 hours

Entry Fee: Only for businesses

Prizes: Trophies and awards

Age Categories: Youth and Adult

Competition Categories: Open

Comments: The Commodores Club is quite proud of its sandcastle contest, which is now in its twenty-eighth year—the oldest contest on the West Coast. The contest is held at Corona Del Mar State Park and offers a great day of fun for the master builder and the novice.

For More Information:

Sandcastle Contest
Newport Beach
Chamber of Commerce
1470 Jamboree Road
Newport Beach, CA 92660

Newport Beach Chamber of Commerce

Date: Late September

Sponsor: Orange County Chapter of the American Institute of Architects

Plot Size: 20' x 20'

Time Allowed: 5 hours

Entry Fee: Yes

Prizes: Awards for the top three teams in two categories

Age Categories: Adult

Competition Categories: Sandcastle and Sand Sculpture

Comments: Proceeds from the contest go to the Orange County Chapter of the American Institute of Architects, which is actively involved in local, state, and national projects ranging from energy conservation to educational scholarships. Sandcastling workshops often preceed this very popular contest.

For More Information:

Sandcastle Contest
Jeff Smith
13028 Parton
Santa Ana, CA 92707

Jeff Smith

Date: Mid July

Sponsor: San Clemente Ocean Festival

Plot Size: 20' x 20'

Time Allowed: 5 hours

Entry Fee: Yes

Prizes: Trophies and awards

Age Categories: Youth and Adult

Competition Categories: Several

Comments: This contest is part of the week-long San Clemente Ocean Festival, and often attracts crowds into the tens of thousands. Sandcastling workshops preceed the contest. Advance registration for the contest is recommended.

For More Information:

Sandcastle Contest
San Clemente
Ocean Festival
P. O. Box 3023
San Clemente, CA 92672

Joey Leno

Date: Early to mid July (see comments)

Sponsor: Community of Ocean Beach

Plot Size: 20' x 20'

Time Allowed: 3 hours

Entry Fee: None

Prizes: Awards in all categories

Age Categories: Youth and Adult

Competition Categories: King of the Castle, Best Free Form, and The Zoo

Comments: The San Diego Sand Sculpturing Championship is relatively new. Mike Stewart, well-known for his work with Sand Sculptors International, designed this contest as a tune-up for the U.S. Open, which usually follows this contest by two weeks.

For More Information:

San Diego Sandsculpturing
Championships
4939 Muir Avenue
San Diego, CA 92107

Warren Blakely

Imperial Beach, California

Date: Varies, depending on time of an extreme low tide; has been held in July the past few years; 1990 contest set for August 5.

Sponsor: Varies from year to year

Plot Size: Varies with category

Time Allowed: 5 hours for Masters; 4 hours for others

Entry Fee: Yes

Prizes: Cash awards and trophies ($5,000 for first place in Masters category)

Age Categories: Youth and Adult

Competition Categories: Masters, Castle of Your Mind, Executive Sandbox, Best Replica, Best Sculpture, and Creatures of the Sea

Comments: The U.S. Open Sandcastle Contest is the premier sandcastling contest in North America. Attendance often reaches 100,000. Advance registration is highly recommended.

For More Information:

U.S. Open
Sandcastle Contest
P. O. Box 476
Imperial Beach, CA 92032

Jerry Barlow

Date: Sometime in February

Sponsor: The University of Hawaii School of Architecture

Plot Size: Open

Time Allowed: 2 hours

Entry Fee: None

Prizes: Awards and trophies

Age Categories: Adult only

Competition Categories: Open

Comments: This very popular contest on a relatively small beach is open to all architectural students, practicing local architects, and faculty from the University of Hawaii School of Architecture. This is a contest known for its creative sculptures.

For More Information:

Sandcastle Contest
U. of Hawaii at Manoa
School of Architecture
George Annex B-3
2560 Campus Road
Honolulu, HI 96822

Gordon Tyau

Date: Mid September

Sponsor: Waikiki Aloe and Spotlight Hawaii

Plot Size: 10' x 10'

Time Allowed: 3 hours

Entry Fee: None

Prizes: Cash awards

Age Categories: Youth and Adult

Competition Categories: Open

Comments: The Hawaiian Open is fast becoming the premier contest of the Islands. Look for more categories to be added in the future. Contestants may participate in teams of one to five members.

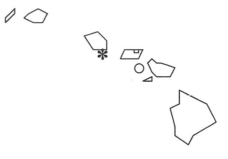

For More Information:

The Hawaiian Open
Sandcastle Championships
2301 Kuhio Avenue
Honolulu, HI 96815

David Watersun

Date: Early May

Sponsor: Central Arizona Chapter of the
American Institute of Architects

Plot Size: Open

Time Allowed: 2.5 hours

Entry Fee: Yes

Prizes: Awards and trophies

Age Categories: Adult

Competition Categories: Open

Comments: This is another inland contest, but with a bit of a twist. The contest is held at the Big Surf Wave Park. Teams may consist of three to five members, but space limits the number of teams that may enter the contest to fifteen.

For More Information:

Sandcastle Contest
Central Arizona
Chapter of the A. I. A.
802 North 5th Street
Phoenix, AZ 85003

Noel West

South Padre Island, Texas

Date: Early October

Sponsor: South Padre Island
Chamber of Commerce

Plot Size: Not specified

Time Allowed: 4 hours

Entry Fee: Yes

Prizes: Cash awards and prizes ($1,500
first place prize in Master category)

Age Categories: Youth and Adult

Competition Categories: Masters, Solo,
Corporate, Family, and Youth

Comments: The South Padre Island Chamber of
Commerce hosts a multitude of sandcastling contests throughout the year, including
a "sandman building" contest held on Val-
entine's Day. For years, South Padre held
the world record for the longest sandcastle—
1.85 miles.

For More Information:

Sandcastle Contest
South Padre Island
Visitor & Convention Center
P. O. Box 3500
So. Padre Island, TX 78597

Walter McDonald

Date: Third weekend in June

Sponsor: C101 Radio and Miller Beer

Plot Size: 20' x 20'

Time Allowed: (see Comments)

Entry Fee: Yes

Prizes: Cash and trophies

Age Categories: Adult

Competition Categories: Open

Comments: The Fourteenth Annual Corpus Christi Contest is a fund-raiser for the Texas Special Olympics. Contestants may start as early as the midnight before. The contest ends at two o'clock the following afternoon.

For More Information:

Sandcastle Contest
C101 Radio
P. O. Box 9781
Corpus Christi, TX 78469

Grain Assault

Date: Early June

Sponsor: Houston Chapter of the American Institute of Architects

Plot Size: 25' x 25'

Time Allowed: 4 hours

Entry Fee: Yes

Prizes: Trophies and awards

Age Categories: Adult and Special Youth Category for 12 years of age and younger

Competition Categories: Open

Comments: The American Institute of Architects Steelcase Sandcastle Competition is open to all design-related professionals. Each firm represented is asked to pay a $500 entry fee to help provide scholarships and promote architectural and environmental awareness.

For More Information:

Sandcastle Competition
Houston Chapter, A.I.A.
20 Greenway Plaza, #246
Houston, TX 77046

Gerald Morehead

Tulsa, Oklahoma

Date: Mid to late July

Sponsors: River Parks Authority and the
American Institute of Architects

Plot Size: 10' x 10'

Time Allowed: 3 hours

Entry Fee: No

Prizes: Trophies

Age Categories: Youth and Adult

Competition Categories: Open

Comments: The Tulsa Contest, which takes place
on the Tulsa River, is one of the most
original contests in North America and also
one of the most popular ones. All sandcastling equipment must be carried by one person in one trip to the plot.

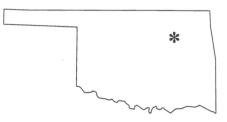

For More Information:

Arkansas River
Sandcastle Contest
River Parks Authority
707 South Houston, #202
Tulsa, OK 74127

River Parks Authority

Biloxi, Mississippi

Date: Third Saturday in September
Sponsor: *The Sun Herald*
Plot Size: 20' x 20'
Time Allowed: 5 hours
Entry Fee: Yes
Prizes: $3,000 in cash awards and trophies
Age Categories: Youth and Adult
Competition Categories: A new theme each year
Comments: The Biloxi Contest is truly a sand sculpturing contest in that no forms and molds are allowed. Teams are limited to five builders. This popular contest has gained media coverage, and advance registration is highly recommended.

For More Information:

Sandcastle Contest
John McFarland,
Marketing Director
The Sun Herald
P. O. Box 4567
Biloxi, MS 39535

The Sun Herald

St. Petersburg, Florida

Date: Late June

Sponsor: The Don CeSar Resort Hotel

Plot Size: 20' x 20'

Time Allowed: Up to 8 hours

Entry Fee: Yes

Prizes: Trophies and awards; Grand Prize winner gets three days and two nights at the Don CeSar Resort Hotel

Age Categories: Youth and Adult

Competition Categories: Several, including Best Replica of the Don CeSar Resort Hotel

Comments: The Don Sandcastle Contest is one of Florida's most popular sandcastling contests, and the competition is always stiff. Every participant receives a complimentary T-shirt. A Masters category is currently being planned.

For More Information:

The Don Sandcastle Contest
c/o Glynna Hanchette
The Don CeSar Resort Hotel
3400 Gulf Boulevard
St. Petersburg Beach, FL
33706

The Don CeSar

Fort Myers Beach, Florida

Date: Veterans Day Weekend

Sponsor: Greater Fort Myers Chamber of Commerce

Plot Size: Open

Time Allowed: 6 hours

Entry Fee: Yes

Prizes: Trophies and awards

Age Categories: Youth and Adult

Competition Categories: Pairs, Teams of 3-4 Members, and Businesses

Comments: The Fort Myers Sandcastle Contest is one of the latest contests to take place in the calendar year. Sandcastling workshops normally preceed the contest and are conducted by Master Builder Michael Di Persio. Held on a beautiful white sandy beach in a pleasant November climate, this is an extremely popular contest. Advance registration is required.

For More Information:

Sandcastle Contest
Greater Fort Myers
Chamber of Commerce
P.O. Box 6109
Fort Myers Beach, FL
33932

The Allen Group

Date: During the Month of May

Sponsor: Holiday Isle Resort & Marina

Plot Size: 20' x 20'

Time Allowed: 6 hours

Entry Fee: Yes (see comments)

Prizes: Trophies and awards

Age Categories: Youth and Adult

Competition Categories: Open

Comments: Located in the Florida Keys, the Islamorada Contest is a fund-raiser to benefit the Coral Shores High School Scholarship Fund. Businesses are asked to donate $150 for each five-member team and $35 for each individual participant.

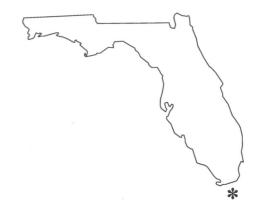

For More Information:

Sandcastle Contest
Chris Bontempo, Coordinator
Holiday Isle Resort & Marina
84001 Overseas Highway
Islamorada, FL 33036

Heather Blades

——Ft. Lauderdale Beach, Florida——

Date: Fourth of July

Sponsor: *News/Sun Sentinel* and the Fort Lauderdale Park and Recreation Department

Plot Size: Juniors: 10' x 10'; Adult: 20' x 20'

Time Allowed: 4 hours

Entry Fee: Yes

Prizes: Cash award ($1,500.00 for first place in the Championship Division)

Age Categories: Youth and Adult

Competition Categories: Champion, Open, and Junior Divisions

Comments: The Fort Lauderdale contest, which has been held for thirty-seven years, is North America's oldest contest. Crowds often top 100,000 for this widely publicized event. Because the competition is limited to one hundred teams, preregistration is recommeded.

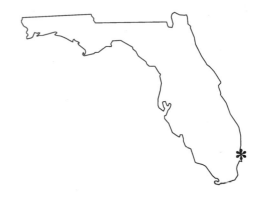

For More Information:

Sand Blast
News/Sun Sentinel
301 North Andrews Ave.
Ft. Lauderdale, FL 33301

News/Sun Sentinel

Date: Last Saturday in July

Sponsor: Delray Beach Sunrise Kiwanis

Plot Size: Open

Time Allowed: 4 hours

Entry Fee: None

Prizes: Team Effort, Best Individual Effort, Best Effort by Participant under Age 15

Age Categories: Youth and Adult

Competition Categories: Open

Comments: This contest is part of the Annual Delray Beach Festival, which also includes volleyball, treasure hunting, kite flying, and life guard and sail board competitions. Team competition is being added as a competition category.

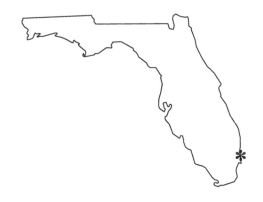

For More Information:

Sandcastle Contest
Kiwanis Club
of Delray Beach
P. O. Box 1963
Delray Beach, FL 33444

Heather Blades

Vero Beach, Florida

Date: Early to mid-August
Sponsor: Vero Beach Jaycees
Plot Size: 10' x 10'
Time Allowed: 3 hours
Entry Fee: Yes
Prizes: Trophies
Age Categories: Open to all ages
Competition Categories: Open
Comments: This recent newcomer to the sand-castle contest circuit is well planned and well executed. Look for it to grow as word spreads of its existence. Proceeds from the contest go to benefit the Vero Beach Jay-cees' scholarship programs.

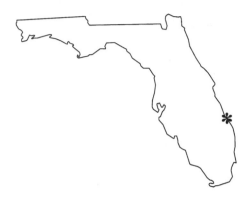

For More Information:

Sandcastle Contest
Rich Luke
650 25th Street SW
Vero Beach, FL 32962

Heather Blades

Date: July

Sponsor: Mid-Florida Brevard Section of the American Institue of Architects

Plot Size: No limit

Time Allowed: 4 hours

Entry Fee: Yes

Prizes: Weekend packages, trophies, and T-shirts

Age Categories: Youth and Adult

Competition Categories: Open

Comments: The Satellite Beach Contest is limited to twenty-five teams, but there is no limit to the number of members on a team. Advance registration is recommended.

For More Information:

Sandcastle Contest
Randy Throng
3275 Pineda Drive
Melbourne, FL 32940

Heather Blades

Cocoa Beach, Florida

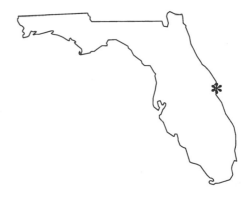

Date: Mid-May

Sponsor: Tourism and Convention Council of Cocoa Beach

Plot Size: 20' x 20'

Time Allowed: 5 hours

Entry Fee: Yes

Prizes: Cash and other prizes

Age Categories: Youth and Adult

Competition Categories: Masters, Youth, and Family

Comments: This sandcastle contest, held during the Cocoa Beach Festival, is just one of many activities on this beautiful Florida beach. Cash prizes up to $2,000 make advance registration advisable.

For More Information:

Sandcastle Contest
Tourism & Convention Council
Cocoa Beach
Chamber of Commerce
400 Fortenberry Road
Merritt Island, FL 32952

Heather Blades

New Smyrna Beach, Florida

Date: Late June or early July

Sponsor: City of New Smyrna Beach

Plot Size: Open

Time Allowed: Up to 7 hours

Entry Fee: None

Prizes: Yes

Age Categories: Youth and Adult

Competition Categories: Sandcastle and Free Form

Comments: Because spectators may drive their cars up and down traffic lanes on the beach during the contest, sand sculptures must face the traffic lanes.

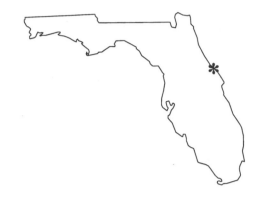

For More Information:

New Smyrna
Sandcastle Contest
c/o Richard Varano
Sea World of Florida
7007 Sea World Drive
Orlando, FL 32821

Jim Richardson

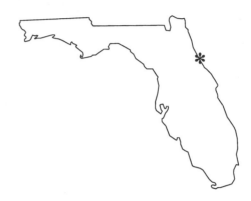

Date: In March (spring break)

Sponsor: Party Smart (Drinking in Moderation & Responsible Consumption)—headquartered in Costa Mesa, California

Plot Size: 10' x 20'

Time Allowed: 4 hours

Entry Fee: None

Prizes: Cash prizes for 1st, 2nd, and 3rd places of $1,000, $750, and $500 respectively, with duplicate amounts going to the scholarship fund of each college represented by the winners; other prizes and awards.

Age Categories: Adult

Competition Categories: Open

Comments: The Daytona Beach Contest is held in conjunction with the college spring break. The tremendous success of the first contest held last year indicates that this contest will soon gain national recognition.

For More Information:

Party Smart
Sandcastle Contest
150 Paularino Ave., #190
Costa Mesa, CA 92626

Totally In Sand

Jacksonville Beach, Florida

Date: Late April/early May

Sponsor: Jacksonville Beach Recreation Department, *The Sun Times*, and *The Beach Leader*

Plot Size: 10' x 10'

Time Allowed: 2.5 hours

Entry Fee: No

Prizes: Free T-Shirts for All Participants

Age Categories: Youth, Adult, and Family

Competition Categories: Open

Comments: A maximum of three people are allowed to a plot, except for the family category, which allows five.

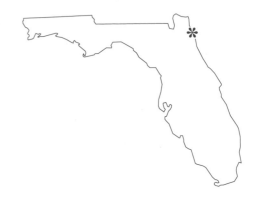

For More Information:

Sandcastle Contest
Recreation Department
City of Jacksonville Beach
11 North Third Street
Jacksonville Beach,
FL 32250

Heather Blades

—Myrtle Beach, South Carolina—

Date: First week in June

Sponsor: Myrtle Beach Area Chamber
of Commerce

Plot Size: (see Comments)

Time Allowed: All day

Entry Fee: None

Prizes: Cash awards and prizes

Age Categories: Open to all ages

Comments: Each year Myrtle Beach sponsors an
event to build the world's longest sandsculpture. In 1989, over 1,200 volunteers
banded together to build a sandcastle 2.85
miles long, beating the current world record. Volunteers are also welcome to join
with professional builders to compete for
the record.

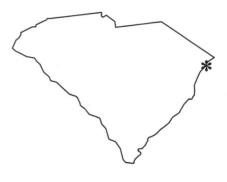

For More Information:

World Record Sandsculpture
Myrtle Beach Area
Chamber of Commerce
P.O. Box 2115
Myrtle Beach, SC 29578

Myrtle Beach Area Chamber of Commerce

—Surfside Beach, South Carolina—

Date: First week in June

Sponsor: South Strand Sertoma Club

Plot Size: 20' x 20'

Time Allowed: 4 hours

Entry Fee: None

Prizes: Yes

Age Categories: Youth and Adult

Competition Categories: Open

Comments: The Surfside Contest is also part of the week-long Sun Fun Festival held at Myrtle Beach.

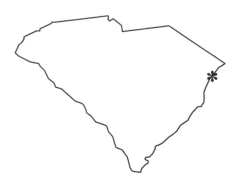

For More Information:

Sandcastle Contest
Sylvia Singleton
South Strand
Sertoma Club
5730 Highway 707—Lot 22
Myrtle Beach, SC 29577

Myrtle Beach Area Chamber of Commerce

—North Myrtle Beach, South Carolina—

Date: First week in June
Sponsor: Optimist Club
Plot Size: Open
Time Allowed: 4 hours
Entry Fee: None
Prizes: Yes
Age Categories: Youth and Adult
Competition Categories: Open
Comments: The North Myrtle Beach Contest is part of the week-long Sun Fun Festival. With nearby Myrtle Beach hosting annual attempts at the world record, this contest is destined to grow in popularity. A good contest for the novice builder.

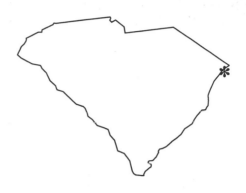

For More Information:

Sandcastle Contest
Optimist Club
Chappell Dew
411 Main Street
North Myrtle Beach,
SC 29582

Jim Richardson

Date: Early August

Sponsor: Shenandoah Acres Resort

Plot Size: Open

Time Allowed: 4 hours

Entry Fee: None

Prizes: Awards and trophies

Age Categories: Youth and Adult

Competition Categories: Open

Comments: This inland contest takes place at the foot of the Blue Ridge Mountains, one of the finest vacation areas on the eastern seaboard.

For More Information:

Sandcastle Contest
Shenandoah Acres Resort
P.O. Box 300
Stuarts Draft, VA 24477

Shenandoah Acres Resort

Date: Mid-August

Sponsor: C and P Yellow Pages

Plot Size: Open

Time Allowed: 3 hours

Entry Fee: None

Prizes: Trophies and awards

Age Categories: Youth and Adult

Competition Categories: Three

Comments: This contest is considered an important tune-up for the much larger Sandcastle Classic held at the same beach during the Neptune Festival. Over 135 sandcastles were built for this contest in 1989. Advance registration is recommended.

For More Information:

Sandcastle Contest
Nancy Moore
City of Virginia Beach
Resort Programs
302 22nd Street
Virginia Beach, VA 23451

Date: Late September

Sponsor: Neptune Festival

Plot Size: Masters, 30' x 30'; Others, 28' x 28'

Time Allowed: 4-5 hours

Entry Fee: Yes

Prizes: Cash awards and trophies; first prize $2,000 in Masters category

Age Categories: Youth and Adult

Competition Categories: Several

Comments: Established in 1974, the Neptune Contest is considered by many to be the premier contest on the East Coast. Masters teams are limited to eight builders and one alternate. Advance registration is recommended.

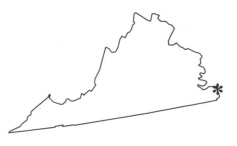

For More Information:

Sandcastle Classic
Virginia Beach
Neptune Festival
265 Kings Grant Road, #102
Virginia Beach, VA 23452

Ocean City, Maryland

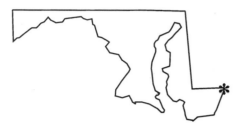

Date: Late June

Sponsor: Castle in Sand Hotel, 100 KHI Radio, and *The Beachcomber* newspaper

Plot Size: 20' x 20'

Time Allowed: 4 hours

Entry Fee: None

Prizes: Trophies and prizes; Grand Prize winner gets a three-night vacation at the Castle in the Sand.

Age Categories: Youth and Adult

Competition Categories: Open

Comments: Now in its twenty-third year, the Ocean City contest has gained wide community support. Along with its annual sandcastling competition, Ocean City is organizing an attempt to beat the world record sandsculpture for height.

For More Information:

Sandcastle Contest
Castle in the Sand Hotel
P.O. Box 190
Ocean City, MD 21842

Castle in the Sand Hotel

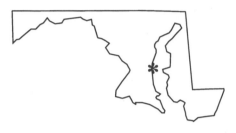

Date: Early September
Sponsor: Maryland Seafood Festival
  and Annapolis Chamber of Commerce
Plot Size: 20' x 20'
Time Allowed: 2 hours
Entry Fee: Yes
Prizes: Cash awards and trophies;
  1st, 2nd, & 3rd places win $200, $100,
  and $50 respectively.
Age Categories: Youth and Adult
Competition Categories: Open
Comments: The Annapolis contest is a fairly new
  competition. The planners are instituting
  changes that should turn this contest into a
  much larger event.

For More Information:

Sandcastle Contest
Maryland Seafood Festival
Six Dock Street
Annapolis, MD 21401

Noel West

Date: Early August

Sponsor: *The Whale* newspaper

Plot Size: 20' x 20'

Time Allowed: 3 hours

Entry Fee: None

Prizes: Cash awards and prizes

Age Categories: Youth and Adult

Competition Categories: Sandcastles, Free-form, and Whales

Comments: The Whale Contest, now in its twelfth year, is a very popular contest. Advance registration is recommended.

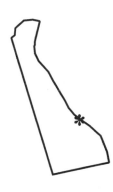

For More Information:

The Whale
Sandcastle Contest
P.O. Box 37
Lewes, DE 19958

The Whale Newspaper

Delaware Seashore St. Park, Delaware

Date: Mid-July
Sponsor: Parks and Recreation Department
Plot Size: 15' x 15'
Time Allowed: 3 hours
Entry Fee: None
Prizes: Trophies and awards
Age Categories: Youth and Adult
Competition Categories: Open
Comments: This small, family-oriented contest
is great for children and the novice
builder. The contest is held at the South-
east Day Area (the south side of the inlet)

For More Information:

Sandcastle Contest
Jack Goins
Parks & Recreation Dept.
P. O. Box 1401
Dover, DE 19903

Heather Blades

Date: July, August, & October (see Comments)
Sponsor: Ocean City Chamber of Commerce
Plot Size: Open
Time Allowed: 2-3 hours
Entry Fee: None
Prizes: Trophies and awards
Age Categories: Youth and Adult
Competition Categories: Open and Groups
    (limited to three persons)
Comments: Ocean City hosts a multitude of sandcastling contests throughout the summer and fall, the largest taking place in August. Sculptors are limited to the use of buckets and shovels.

For More Information:

Sandcastle Contest
Mark Soifer
Public Relations Dept.
City Hall
9th & Asbury Avenue
Ocean City, NJ 08226

Ocean City Public Relations Department

Date: Late July

Sponsor: Bally's Grand Casino Hotel

Plot Size: Open

Time Allowed: 4 hours

Entry Fee: None

Prizes: Trophies and awards; grand prize—three days, two nights at Bally's Grand Hotel; free T-shirts for pre-registered contestants.

Age Categories: Youth and Adult

Competition Categories: Sandsculpture or Sandcastle

Comments: Now in its tenth year, the Bally's Grand Sand Castle Contest is destined to become a major event. Advance registration is recommended for this very popular contest. Teams may consist of two to four people.

For More Information:

Sandcastle Contest
c/o Muriel Harris
Public Relations
Boston & Pacific Avenues
Atlantic City, NJ 08404

Heather Blades

Date: August
Sponsor: Concerned Taxpayers Association
Plot Size: Open
Time Allowed: Up to 8 hours
Entry Fee: None
Prizes: Trophies
Age Categories: Youth (under 15 years of age) and Adult (15 years of age and older)
Competition Categories: Open
Comments: This is primarily a contest for youth, although it is also popular with adults. A good contest for the solo castler.

For More Information:

Sandcastle Contest
Concerned Taxpayers Assoc.
10 Lowell Avenue
Trenton, NJ 08619

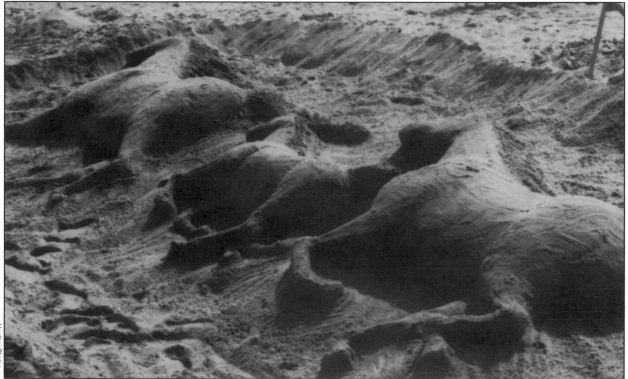

Heather Blades

Belmar, New Jersey

Date: Mid-July

Sponsor: New Jersey Bell Yellow Pages

Plot Size: Open

Time Allowed: 3 hours

Entry Fee: None

Prizes: Trophies and awards for Most Creative, Tallest, and the Most Towers

Age Categories: Youth and Adult

Competition Categories: Open

Comments: Even though this contest is only four years old, its supporters expect it to take its place among the other major contests held on the East Coast.

For More Information:

Sandcastle Contest
Popple Tyson/
Jennifer Alexander
201 Littleton Road
Morris Plains, NJ 07950

Richard Varano

208

Date: August

Sponsor: Milford Fine Arts Council and
Milford Recreation Department

Plot Size: 15' x 15'

Time Allowed: 3 hours

Entry Fee: Yes

Prizes: Awards in each category;
cash awards for the best entries

Age Categories: Youth and Adult

Competition Categories: Individual, Family,
Group, and Clubs

Comments: Now fifteen years old, The Great
American Sandcastle and Sculpture Contest is held at Silver Sands State Park.
Because the contest is widely publicized
in print and on television, advance registration is recommended.

For More Information:

The Great American
Sandcastle & Sculpture
Contest
c/o William Meddick
5 Broad Street
Milford, CT 06460

Heather Blades

Narragansett, Rhode Island

Date: Late August
Sponsor: Narragansett Parks
    and Recreation Department
Plot Size: Small
Time Allowed: Under 4 hours
Entry Fee: None
Prizes: Ribbons for each category;
    trophy for best overall entry
Age Categories: Several youth categories;
    Adult category
Competition Categories: Individual and Group
Comments: This family-oriented contest emphasizes participation rather than competition. An excellent event for the novice builder.

For More Information:

Sandcastle Competition
Narragansett Parks
& Recreation Department
25 5th Avenue
Narragansett, RI 02882

Date: Mid to late August

Sponsor: Nantucket Island Chamber of Commerce and the Nantucket Island School of Design and the Arts

Plot Size: Open

Time Allowed: 3 hours

Entry Fee: Small entry fee

Prizes: Trophies and awards

Age Categories: Youth and Adult

Competition Categories: Youth, Family, Individual, and Adult

Comments: The Nantucket Beach Contest is held at Jetties Beach. This seventeen-year-old contest is very popular for both children and families.

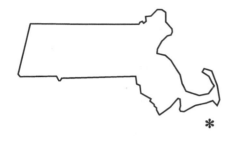

*

For More Information:

Sandcastle Contest
Nantucket Island
Chamber of Commerce
Nantucket Island, MA 02554

Nantucket Island Chamber of Commerce

—South Yarmouth, Massachusetts—

Date: Mid-August and early October

Sponsor: Yarmouth Seaside Festival and
South Yarmouth Chamber of Commerce

Plot Size: 20' x 20'

Time Allowed: 3 hours

Entry Fee: None

Prizes: Awards

Age Categories: Youth and Adult

Comments: South Yarmouth sponsors two
sandcastling events. Both are great contests for the novice builder and for children.

For More Information:

Sandcastle Contest
South Yarmouth
Chamber of Commerce
P. O. Box 479
South Yarmouth, MA 02664

Susan Kusanich

Date: Early August

Sponsor: Ipswich Parks and Recreation Depart.

Plot Size: 20' x 40' to 40' x 40'

Time Allowed: 2 hours

Entry Fee: No

Prizes: Certificates

Age Categories: Open to children only

Competition Categories: Open

Comments: Ipswich hosts two very different and very large contests. This first contest usually involves over 1,200 children. For information about the contest for adults (usually held in mid-August), write: Cranes Beach; Trustees of the Reservation; Argilla Road; Ipswich, MA 01938

For More Information:

Sandcastle Contest
Ipswich Parks &
Recreation Department
23 Central Street
Ipswich, MA 01938

Ipswich Park and Recreation Department

—Hampton Beach, New Hampshire—

Date: Early August

Sponsor: Hampton Beach Chamber of Commerce

Plot Size: Open

Time Allowed: 3 hours

Entry Fee: None

Prizes: Trophies and awards

Age Categories: Youth only

Competition Categories: Four categories for children and youths

Comments: The Hampton Beach Contest is part of a three-day children's festival. With four youth categories plus face painting, a children's parade, and free ice cream, how could this contest be anything but popular?

For More Information:

Sandcastle Contest
Visitor Information Center
180 Ocean Boulevard
Hampton Beach, NH 03842

Date: In August

Sponsor: Wells Area Chamber of Commerce

Plot Size: 20' x 20'

Time Allowed: Up to 4 hours

Entry Fee: None

Prizes: Awards and trophies

Age Categories: Youth and Adult

Competition Categories: Open

Comments: The Wells Sandcastle Contest began as a demonstration to the citizens of Wells that the harbor needed to be dredged. The harbor's condition was so bad that sandcastles could be built in the middle of it. The harbor has been dredged, and now every August sandcastles are built on the beach instead of in the middle of the harbor.

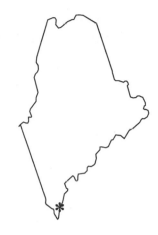

For More Information:

Sandcastle Contest
Wells Area
Chamber of Commerce
P.O. Box 356
Wells, ME 04090

Jim Richardson

Old Orchard Beach, Maine

Date: Third weekend in August

Sponsor: Old Orchard Beach Chamber of Commerce

Plot Size: Not specified

Time Allowed: 3 hours

Entry Fee: None

Prizes: Awards

Age Categories: Youth and Adult divisions

Competition Categories: Several

Comments: Named after an old apple orchard that served as a landmark for sailors, the tiny town of Old Orchard has been known to welcome over 100,000 during its annual sandcastle contest. The contest is part of an annual fundraising effort for the Maine Special Olympics and takes place over the entire weekend.

For More Information:

Sandcastle Contest
c/o Beach Olympics
P. O. Box 587
Old Orchard Beach, ME 04064

Roger Dubé

Date: Late June

Sponsor: New England Telephone Company

Plot Size: 20' x 20'

Time Allowed: 2 hours

Entry Fee: None

Prizes: Awards

Age Categories: Youth and Adult

Competition Categories: Open

Comments: The Portland Sandcastle Contest is part of the Spring Point Festival and is held annually at Willard Beach.

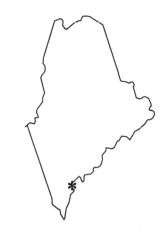

For More Information:

Sandcastle Contest
Spring Point Festival
142 Free Street
Portland, ME 04101

Heather Blades

Date: Late July

Sponsor: Wayne County Parks System and the Detroit Chapter of the American Institute of Architects

Plot Size: 20' x 15'

Time Allowed: 3 hours

Entry Fee: Yes

Prizes: Winner receives the coveted "We're Building Sandcastles in the Sand" trophy.

Age Categories: Adult

Competition Categories: Open

Comments: Presently this contest is being held at the volleyball courts at Nankin Hills with sand that has been trucked in. Future plans include moving the contest to the beach in order to accomodate the tremendous increases in attendance.

For More Information:

Sandcastle Contest
Wayne County Parks System
33175 Ann Arbor Trail
Westland, MI 48185

Ben Tiseo

Date: First Saturday in June

Sponsor: Chicago Chapter of the
American Institute of Architects

Plot Size: Open

Time Allowed: 4 hours

Entry Fee: None

Prizes: Trophies and awards

Age Categories: Youth and Adult

Competition Categories: Different theme
picked each year

Comments: This Midwest contest is well-organized and very popular. This event is open
to A.I.A. and non-A.I.A participants. Advance registration is recommended.

For More Information:

Sandcastle Contest
Chicago Chapter A.I.A.
53 West Jackson, Suite 350
Chicago, IL 60604

M.B. Carrol

Date: Mid-July

Sponsor: 58 CKY Radio

Plot Size: Open

Time Allowed: 4 hours

Entry Fee: Yes

Prizes: Gifts, trophies, and awards

Age Categories: Youth and Adult

Competition Categories: Open

Comments: This contest in the past has served as an effective fundraiser for the local children's hospital.

For More Information:

Sandcastle Contest
58 CKY Radio
Polo Park
Winnepeg, MB R3G 0L7
Canada

Totally In Sand

More Contests

The following communities also host (or are planning to host) sandcastle contests. Complete information was not available when this book went to press.

Blaine, Washington: Look for a contest in Blaine by 1992. Blaine Chamber of Commerce; 9261 Semiahmoo Parkway; Blaine, WA 98230.

Morro Bay, California: Morro Bay will host an annual contest starting in 1991. Morro Bay Recreation Department; 1001 Kennedy Way; Morro Bay, CA 93442.

Santa Rosa, California: The Redwood Empire American Institute of Architects hosts an annual contest. Redwood Empire A. I. A.; P.O. Box 4178; Santa Rosa, CA 95402.

Manhattan Beach, California: Manhattan Beach hosts an annual contest. Manhattan Beach Park Department; Phone: (213) 545-5621.

Oxnard, California: Oxnard hosts an annual contest. Channel Island Harbor Association of Leases; 3600 South Harbor Boulevard, Suite 215; Oxnard, CA 93035.

Lahaina, Hawaii: The 505 Front Street Mall hosts an occasional contest. 505 Front Street Mall; Phone: (808) 667-2514

Kahului, Hawaii: The local chapter of the American Institute of Architects hosts an annual contest. Phone (808) 531-7134.

Gulf Shores, Alabama: Gulf Shores hosts an annual contest. Gulf Shores Chamber of Commerce; P.O. Drawer 457, Gulf Shores, AL 36547.

Siesta Key, Florida: The Siesta Key Chamber of Commerce hosts an annual contest. Siesta Key Chamber of Commerce; 5263 Ocean Boulevard; P.O. Box 35400; Siesta Key, FL 34242.

Orlando, Florida: The Florida State Championships will begin 1991. Rich Varano; c/o SeaWorld of Florida, Entertainment Department; 7007 Sea World Drive; Orlando, FL 32821.

Savannah, Georgia: Savannah hosts an annual contest. Paul Mezo; 8 Mall Court, Suite 6; Savannah, GA 31406.

Ocracoke, North Carolina: Ocracoke hosts an annual contest. Ocracoke Chamber of Commerce; Phone (919)928-6711.

What Holds Sandcastles Together

When you have had the opportunity to castle on several beaches, you will notice distinct differences in how the sand behaves. You can build successfully to a height of ten feet on one beach, but may be able to reach only eight feet somewhere else. A similar structure might stand twelve feet at yet another beach. The difference is partly due to the shape and size of the sand grains, and partly to the content of the sand. Sand that is continually pounded by surf, rolling in and out with the tide, gradually becomes rounded and smaller in size. Sand grains found in the protected waters of a lake or sound might have a more jagged shape and might be a little larger. Since the surface planes are generally larger, grains with the jagged shape "interlock" better than spherical grains, making the structure more resistant to collapse.

When a sandcastle collapses, it does not topple over like a felled tree. A portion of the structure shears off on the side where the most stress is applied. It is very much like what happens in an avalanche of snow. Sand, like a snowpack, has what is called an angle of dynamic friction: it can pile up only so far before it "slides" down again. How steep that angle is, and how much weight the structure will support before it gives way, depends on the shape and cohesiveness of the grains in the structure. That means that different types of sand will hold together better than others, and will support taller, steeper constructions. Extremely coarse sand cannot be used to build very tall structures, since the angle of dynamic friction for coarse sand is relatively shallow. The sand grains are subjected to a stronger gravitational force, which the cohesive forces cannot compensate for. Once the angle of dynamic friction for your building material is passed, your structure is doomed. Brace yourself for the sandcastler's disaster.

Two cohesive forces help wet grains of sand—and therefore your sandcastle—stick together. The first is surface tension, the attraction between water molecules that gives water a skin, and causes it to bead up on a freshly waxed car. As that attraction works between the water molecules, it tends to bring along for the ride whatever grains of sand happen to be in the way.

The second cohesive force is ionic bonding, the attraction between particles with negative and positive electrical charges. Dry sand grains naturally repel each other because their surfaces all have the same negative charge. That is why a handful of dry sand seems so loose, and why the grains tend to escape between your fingers. Once wet, however, the sand grains form a double layer of ionic charge called a Helmholtz double layer. This electrical force is very weak, except at the surface. There the force is strong enough to hold sand together—as long as the moisture is present. Very small sand grains, interestingly enough, cannot generate this double electrical field; castles built with very fine sand erode faster and are subject to more frequent collapses.

The ideal sand for castle building contains a small amount of clay. Sand grains and clay particles differ in many respects. Clay particles are much smaller, are loosely packed, and are platelike in shape. Sand grains pack more firmly against each other, but slide under pressure rather than holding together like the clay particles. Clay alone cannot generate this double layer of ironic bonding because its particles are too small. The shape of clay particles allows them to bend, however, and this elasticity makes a very strong bond. When their talents are combined in the proper proportions, sand and clay make an excellent building material that packs well and is less likely to shear than pure sand. If a good mixture of sand and clay is packed, as it would be in using forms, the pressure helps create stronger ionic bonds between the sand particles. As the moisture evaporates in the structure, it begins to solidify rather than to disintegrate, because the clay particles will fuse to the sand grains.

For More Information

Books and Articles:

Adkins, Jan. *The Art and Industry of Sandcastling*. New York: Walker Publishing, 1971.

Allen, Joseph. *Sandcastles*. New York: Doubleday, 1981.

Di Persio, Michael. *Castles in the Sand*. (Ten projects that can be built in one to six hours.) Created by Michael Di Persio. Text by Jeffrey Shear and Steven Schneider. Photography by Toby Richards. New York: Putnam, 1982.

Lynas, G. Augustine. *Sandsong*. Ed. Marilyn Meyers. New York: St. Martin's Press, 1983.

McDonald, Walter, and Lucinda Wierenga. *Sand Castles Step by Step*. Deephaven, Minnesota: Meadowbrook Press, 1990.

Simo, Connie. *Sandtiquity*. New York: Taplinger Publishing, 1980.

Walker, Jeral. "Why Do Particles of Sand and Mud Stick Together When They Are Wet?" *Scientific American,* no. 246 (January 1982): 174-79.

Wiersma, Pieter. *Chateaux de Sable*. c/o H. Sieben Da Costakade 139, 1053 WT Amsterdam, Holland.

Videos:

Henderson, David. *The Magic of Sandsculpture*. 3422 Waco St. #3, San Diego, Calif., 92117. Walkervision Interarts, 1990.

Lynas, G. Augustine. *Sandsong*. 250 W. 57th St., Ste. 916, New York, N.Y., 10019. Wumbat Films and Video, 16 mm, 1/2 inch video.

Sandcastling Masters:
How To Reach the Experts

Marc Altamar
446 Zelda Blvd.
Daytona Beach, FL 32118
USA
(904) 257 5893

Arch i sands
Greg LeBon, Captain
21321 Stonehaven Lane
El Toro, CA 92630
USA
(714) 855 8091

Artisands Des Dreams
Allan Matsumoto, Captain
253 Rossmore Court
Port Coquitlam, B.C. V3K 5H2
Canada
(604) 936 8309

California Dreamers
Kali Bradford, Captain
517 Dove Circle
Vista, CA 92083
USA
(619) 940 9125

Dawkin's Sculptures
Paul Dawkins
1516—475 Elgin Street
Ottawa, Ontario K2P 2E6
Canada
(613) 233 2530

Michael Di Persio
409 4th Ave.
Bradley Beach, NJ 07720
USA
(201) 988 0100

Freddie and The Sandblasters
Fred Dobbs, Captain
202 Howe Street
Victoria, B.C. V8V 4K6
Canada
(604) 384 3910

The Flying Zambinis
John Danna, Papa Zambini
1470 Pepper Drive
El Cajon, CA 92021
USA
(619) 588 8975

Grain Assault
Darcy Gertz, Captain
1135 B Cartier Ave.
Coquitlam, B.C. V3K 2C2
Canada
(604) 931 6608

The Great Sandinis
Doug Harle, Co-captain
747 E. 9th
North Vancouver, B.C. V7L 2C1
Canada
(604) 980 7032

Gary Kinsella
127 East 9th Ave.
Escondido, CA 92025
USA
(619) 743 2220

Billy Lee
Sandimaginations
P.O. Box 11235
Lahaina, Hawaii (Maui) 96761
USA
(808) 661 8807

G. Augustine Lynas
233 West 83rd St., Apt. 4-A
New York, NY 10024
USA
(212) 799 0675

Joe Maize
310 Lewers
Honolulu, Hawaii (Oahu) 96815
USA
(808) 923 0751

Lars Van Nigtevegt
Schans 18
6852 CX Huissen
Holland
(085) 251684

The Orbital Sanders
Ken Large, Co-captain
215 Columbia
Seattle, WA 98104
USA
(206) 682 1133

Sand Sculptors International—San Diego
Gerry Kirk, Captain
304 Pacific Ave.
Solana Beach, CA 92075
USA
(619) 755 3714

Sandcastles Unlimited
Kent Trollen, Captain
509 31st, Ste. 201
Newport Beach, CA 92663
USA
(714) 673 4417

Sandyhands
Warren Blakely, Captain
2345 Loring St.
San Diego, CA 92109
USA
(619) 483 7439

Sons of the Beach
Walter McDonald, Co-captain
P.O. Box 2694
South Padre Island, TX 79597
USA
(512) 761 5943

Team Hardcore, or
Sand Sculptors International—L.A.
Todd Vander Pluym, Captain
425 Via Anita Way
Redondo Beach, CA 90277
USA
(213) 378 5559

Totally in Sand
Charlie Beaulieu, Captain
19709 27th Ave. N.W.
Richmond Beach, WA 98197
USA
(206) 546 8679

Richard Varano
Sea World of Florida, Entertainment Dept.
7007 Sea World Drive
Orlando, FL 32821
USA
(407) 351 3600 Ext. 169

—— City Index of Contests ——